Aloha La'a Kea
Sacred Light of Love

Edited by Robert Uhene Maikai

Savant Books and Publications
Honolulu, HI, USA
2020

Published in the USA by Savant Books and Publications
2630 Kapiolani Blvd #1601
Honolulu, HI 96826
http://www.savantbooksandpublications.com

Printed in the USA

Edited by Robert Uhene Maikai
Cover by Daniel S. Janik
Cover image ID 1766743 © Hemul | Dreamstime.com

13 digit ISBN: 978-0-9996938-6-5

First Edition: July 2020
Library of Congress Control Number: 2020912076

Dedication
To being alive in trying times.

Acknowledgements

This year's anthology came into being during challenging times, epitomized by the COVID-19 pandemic. People everywhere are being forced to rethink every aspect of society and their individual lives. Without the selfless, tireless assistance of Savant's publisher, Daniel S. Janik, this year's anthology might never have risen above the vicissitudes of the times. I also want to acknowledge the devoted assistance of the numerous native Hawaiian and religious poets who helped bring this work together as an egalitarian praise of life.

Table of Contents

Foreword

When I was selected to be the guest editor for the 2020 Savant Poetry Anthology, I presented Savant with a challenge: In times like these of drastic change, it's all too easy to forget the many blessings we have, the greatest of which is life itself. While in the past, Savant let the poems determine the theme, I've edited this edition with the thought of "praise," namely, praise for that greatest of gifts, life, and the privilege of being alive. Savant has never done a "praise" anthology *per se*, and keeping it non-sectarian and culturally diverse proved quite demanding. Interestingly, while the call for submissions didn't state any theme, most of the poems included in this 2020 anthology are indeed poems of praise in one way or another, as reflected in the anthology title, which was taken from my own native Hawaiian language. It is my hope that this tenth edition of the Savant Poetry Anthology will prove uplifting to every reader's spirit, leaving us all with a profound sense of awe and appreciation for, once again, simply being alive.

- Robert "Uhene" Maikai

Greg Dasalla - The life of the land is perpetuated in righteousness. Stand of a People for Life.

WARRIORS OF O'AHU -- Dedicated to the Warriors of O'ahu who fought and died for what was true.

WHO WE ARE, HAWAIIANS -- Dedicated to the struggling time of Hawaiians in Hawaii

WARRIORS OF O'AHU

As I set my eyes on the ancient cliffs of O'ahu.
It causes me to gaze up upon their might
Just like the ancient warriors of long ago
Who fought to hold what was theirs.

So, why, why, why,
Did it have to end to this way?
Why, why, why,
Did history betray them?

Now only the bloody cliffs know of the warriors of O'ahu
It causes me to see the ancient fights
Of long ago as the ancient warriors did
Who fought to hold what was theirs.

So, why, why why,
Did it have to turn out this way?
Why, why, why,
Did history turn out this way?

Those ancient warriors of long ago
Who fought to the death for their land,
There is no land,
All gone away, into another's hand.

They fought for what was their birthright

To hold the land
But the new warriors
Came and conquered them away.

So why, why, why,
Did it have to come this way?
Why, why, why,
Did history turn away?

WHO WE ARE, HAWAIIANS

Life is so hard when we try to be like them.
Why is it so,
When we try to look like them?
When who we are, here we are, Hawaiians.

Hawaiians. How can our lives be broken every time,
Now look at us,
We are the people of the land
With no land, no future, no hope.

Who we are, who we are, Hawaiians
What can we do
When our life is just headache
We the Hawaiians, the life of land no more.

The life of the land is supposed to be perpetuated in righteousness --
Righteousness?
Who are we, then; who are we?
Hawaiians? Hawaiian?

The life of the land is perpetuated in righteousness.
Ua mau ke ea
Oka aina ika pono.
Who are we, then , who are we?
 Hawaiians! Hawaiians!

Garrett Uehara -- Its here. Do stay awhile and really see the eternal spotlight, that captures the meaning of what existence is all about.

WHAT MORE? -- Dedicated to my dearest love and lifetime partner, my wife, Lynn.

WHAT A STRUGGLE -- Dedicated to my dearest love, my wife, Lynn.

GLORY -- Dedicated to my family, my church and dear, precious wife, Lynn.

WHAT MORE?

Cared over much
Far beyond anything the world can comprehend
Solving correctly
The puzzle of being in new, breathtaking ways
Glorious amazement
Very much of every very bit of gratitude
Stepping out into world
My heart living the divine to broadcast the reality of true love

WHAT A STRUGGLE

I don't really know about anyone else.
But I do so struggle with
The activities of daily life
The world seems so confusing
Hectic situations wait in everyday events
Demanding their toll in struggle,
Just to be
Just to maintain
Represent,
Respond
With from a reasonable
Position --
Any Position --
Which is in many ways not so much a struggle
With the all that happens,
As it is a struggle with my inner self
To bringing
If just or a moment,
Some peace and contentment to my unsettled soul.
Its the little things
Inside
That are constantly begging release
From the struggle of daily realities.
Oh, what a struggle!

GLORY

Sing and praise
Worship
Bless with honor

Sing and praise
Name a name
above all names
Adore the awestruck ways of creation
Its endearingness
Given to help call out
Pull out of the sticky mud
Setting the answer
To the call
To take heed
From above

Sing and praise
Sing and praise

Moses Pilla - Life is quite amazing when considering the its source. It is a challenge to be a light on my own road of peace, safety and comfort, such that others may see the opportunity in their own lives to be the best they can be. Look and see, astounded by it all, always giving gladness and rejoicing in simply being alive.

GO UNTARNISHED, NON-CALLOUS LIFE - Dedicated to friends and family, with special thanks to my men's group. In honor of living without getting conceptually destroyed.

NO TAME ANIMAL PURPOSE IN KICKING OFF CHAINS OF IMPRISONMENT

EVERY LEVEL AND MANNER - Dedicated to all *ohana* (family) all around the world. May the gladness that has been given me be also enjoyed by everyone.

AN UNTARNISHED, NON-CALLOUS LIFE

'Oh my callousness!
Don't want or care to be callous.
Callous in wanting to be really truly free.
Freedom
From my harsh, unfruitful, unappealing days of distortion
Of mind, body, and soul.

Suddenly supercharged
In many things wrongfully calloused
Entrenched in ever so complicated
Distraught
Over disruptions, dissipated by doubt
Bent equations, mistakes unequaled.

Satisfaction in not being
Callous
Demanding hope and inspiration
A fallacy
A big barrel of fallacy
Rather hope and inspiration for others.

Callous in thinking I could emulate
Right and good
To present a pattern after precedent
Thin air
The urges that take precedence
In conduct unable to be handled properly.

Spiraling out of control
Callous towards carrying out a single task
Not at all

Even to ponder in my complicity
A tightly fitted knot
Secured to keep out unnecessary harm.

But now instead it whips
Callously
Around freely to brutally ignite
Severely multiply
The demolishment of all my gains
On a grandeur scale for simply trying.

NO TAME ANIMAL PURPOSE IN KICKING OFF CHAINS OF IMPRISONMENT

Nature is careless,
Steeping its children in uncontrollable desires
And overwhelming appetites.
Out of balance,
Corrupt,
Needing prodding.
As inner cells work their way
outwardly to a whole,
Animal, animal, animal,
Desire slowly subsides
Until
In a substantial contrite change in ways
The wild
Becomes
Tame, tame, tame.
Let one be kept to fight
To never surrender
When despicable conditions
Let out the
Animals, animals, animals
Hoping to care in better ways
Much more deeply.
The qualities of

Tame, tame, and tame
Need to be daily reborn
Refreshed
Renewed
To keep them from the Absurd
One only,
Untamed,
An oasis
For the tame, tame, tame
Animals, animals, animals

EVERY LEVEL AND MANNER

I so need praised
For all I've done
In such a marvelous concrete manner.

I so need meaning
The only right way
So everyone will see sooner, but hopefully not later

I so need to be praised!
For giving adoration fully
Acknowledging the gift of love that is owed me so much

Brought out of the clay
Having surrendered all
I need to hear a voice reciting the breath of life to all
But mostly me

We all so need praised
If nothing else, for getting in shape
Mapping out perplexity

I need to praise
In the highest
In marvelous exultation
That beyond, above, totally far away for every all

Malia Elliott was born and raised on Oahu. A world-traveler and staunch advocate of Hawaiian and family values, she is a music lyric composer, entertainer, storyteller, actress, playing musical comedy to Shakespeare. She co-composed the lyrics and storyline for *Boy with Goldfish* (London Symphony Recording), *Voyage of the Hokule'a* (National Geographic TV Special that won a Drama Critics Award), *Sail On Moana* (Polynesian Voyaging Society Education Resource) *Keiki Calabash*, *Hawaii Kids Calabash* and other Leon & Malia series products.

www.leonandmalia.com and www.hawaiikidsmusic.com

LAND OF THE WHITE WATERFALL - a story-poem for those who wonder if they might have lost ChildSight.

LAND OF THE WHITE WATERFALL: Hope From the Smallest Light

GoodEarth comes when down I seem,
And brings me tea and tales of dreams.
Cry I, Laugh I, while hot leaves stir,
Renewed, my cup now filled with mirth.
Tells he of the land where the Good King and Queen reign,
With Wizard Great who commands tides and growing of grain.
This land be filled with the Little People
Whose hearts are clear and bold,
With Strength to share in active faith.
This timeless Tale of Hope is told.

They work their day beneath Golden Sun
Content in their green fields 'till work is done.
Then to their homes they gladly run
When the Mare of Night prepares to come.
Sitting warm by crackling fire and reading from the Book,
They hear Tales of Ancient Past,
And sing songs of thanks that the Stories will always last.

On days when the Silver Mist falls,
They leave home for honeyed mead in the Great Hall.
There, King and Queen and Wizard Great
Welcome and instruct them all.

17

Queen talks of Love that drips down like golden sand,
And laments for the Ones-Who-Have-Forgotten in the Outer
Land.
"Now, Chosen Ones, begin your march" she tells them clear,
"You know it is our Duty to go there many times a year.
Though we be unknown to Outer-Land-People we can help
Them to see – that Kindness, a Smile and Humility given in
Love is the Key.
We all know that here, but that is why the Outer People do
Not think we are real –they cannot see us – we are so clear.
Yet we still go about our work with them,
Doing good deeds in the World of Men."
Honeyed mead steaming, silver mist falling, little lights
gleaming,
It was time to bid farewell to those who would roam,
While the others returned to their cozy warm homes.

And so it was, as we drank to the end of our sweet fragrant tea,
When GoodEarth smiled and laughed with me.
Then said in voice both full and meek,
"I go home now for a little while, but one of my brothers
will be back when your heart is heavy and you cannot smile".
Happy to agree, I blew the honeyed steam from my tea, and
GoodEarth's light I could clearly see,
As he walked down the darkened pathway alone,

The joined all the other little lights as they headed for Home.

Nicole Maika'i St. Louis - It's time to relax and just take it all in.

NAOLI BY CHANT - Dedicated to my lovely Mom and humorous Dad

PU MAIKA'I - Dedicated to my lovely Mom and humorous Dad

DEDICATED TO GREG C UPON HIS WAY TO AN OLYMPIC CROWN

NAOLI BY CHANT

Maka pi'a pi'a naoli , Maka pi'a pi'a naoli
Take out the maka pi'a pi'a
From the eyes
Take out the maka pi'a pi'a
From the eyes
Sharing Aloha , Sharing the Aloha
Of the tropics of Hawaii nei

In the tropics of Hawaii nei
Give'um the shaka
Give'um da shaka
For our ke Ali'i Aloha
For our ke Ali'i Aloha

PU MAIKA'I

Pu Maika'i pupu ho'oana. Pu Maika'i pupu ho'oana
PU MAIKA'I!
Pu Maika'i pupu ho'oana. Pu Maika'i pupu ho'oana
Aloha ke Akua ho'oana nanea
Aloha ke Akua ho'ona naunea

Ho'omana ke Ali'i mea I
Mea pili mai 'oe. Mea pili mai 'oe
Every things all about love
Every things all about love
Live to praise

All is the one too truly become like always praise
To be involved in daily lives to share love.
Aloha ke Akua ho'oana nanea, Aloha ke Akua ho'ona naunea
Ho'omana ke Ali'i mea I
Mea pili mai 'oe, Mea pili mai 'oe
Every things all about love
Every things all about love

Do live to praise
All is the one too truly become like always praise
To be involved in daily lives to share love and praise.

DEDICATED TO GREG C UPON HIS WAY TO AN OLYMPIC CROWN

So my eyes saw amazement
In his physique,
So resplendently put together!

My eyes saw amazement
In such beauty
So perfectly put together!

So detailed,
Chiseled with deep ingrained lines
That say,
"In your wonderment, be captivated!"

It's as heaven came down
And touched earth's dust,
Giving it a radiance
A shine
That eons of longing individuals
Finally realized.

How eyes see amazement
In something so simple.
Nothing can compare
To such a tantalizing amazement.

Jay Palompo - Make the call and speak the truth

BLOODSPEAK

BLOODSPEAK

Pulled out of the mud,
Completely turn to trust
Guaranteed, certified trust.
Now plead for your life!

Ken Rasti, also known as "Yes" among friends, is a Professor at several universities and a business management consultant for multiple organizations. He recently was inducted into the Heroes of Humanity Hall of Fame in recognition of his positive community contributions with Aloha in the center of his heart.He has had a prose article published title, "Aloha, I Love You, We Are All Connected", in a book titled Messages of Peace. He lives in Hawaii, and has a daughter and a son who live and work in California.

His poems appear in BELLWETHER MESSAGES - 2013 Savant Poetry Anthology, SHADOW AND LIGHT 0 2017 Savant Poetry Anthology and KINDRED - 2018 Savant Poetry Anthology.

TIME IS A TYRANT

A BATTLEFIELD - Dedicated to my Son, Dimitri

STILL STANDING

MERRY NEW YEAR - Dedicated to Ke Akua

ALONE IN ROME - Dedicated to my Daughter, Mitrah

TIME IS A TYRANT

Time is a tyrant
A relentless ticker

I was riding on a merry-go-round
Trying to catch up with Time

Oh, how I want to live in the present moment
…I closed my eyes for a moment
And the moment was gone

I am on the brink of rebellion
Vulnerable to Time
…To darkness in the world
Shall I drink my wine,
And forget about Time?

My mind shuttles back and forth with Time
Let's take the next train
The runaway Train
From tracks of Time

Who can bend Time in my favor?
Together we will forge Time

I look for you through Time
I can wait

Let me feel your presence
Like a warm blanket on a cold night
It feels right

Meet me in the timelessness
In the timelessness of every sunrise, every sunset
I can't wait.

Was Time designed to protect me from me?
Could I bear to see all my life at once?
I can wait

Though Time is unlimited by Time
It is in the present Time that I meet Time

I have journeyed mysterious steep rugged roads
...Wishing I had more Time

Uncertainties along the roads ahead of me
I look neither behind nor before me

Is it possible to curse Time and thank Time at the same time?
Will I find Time at the end of the rainbow?

Time is the ever present of my soul
Travel through Time with me

What Time is it?
Only Time will tell.

A BATTLEFIELD

Does our big world seem like a big battle field?
Does it seem like the big, big forces against us would not
yield?

I heard him say...
I shall not yield
I shall overcome some day

I whispered...
Have you made your life more difficult than it was meant to
be?

He said...
Maybe I have created some obstacles
The path, I could not see
I shall overcome some day

I heard a voiceless cry in the wilderness...
I am looking for a one way highway in the desert
Take me straight to the top of the mountain
It's my way or the highway
I shall overcome some day

Where do you look for solutions?
Where do you find big, big solutions?
He sighed...

I looked for them in our big world, outside
I found them in my big, big world, inside

Love will color the way
I shall not yield
I shall overcome some day

STILL STANDING

Standing on the promises of hope
I shall find strength to cope

Yearning to wash away my fears in the gentle rain
I found myself in the hurricane

Standing on the promises that cannot fail
My boat finds the homeward wind to sail

Standing on the promises of God
In the midst of storms of doubt and fear
The sun and the blue skies are near

Standing on the ladder of hope
With its supports hidden in the Secret Place of the Most High
I step on and up trusting His Hold

I step on and up with my heart
I let my head follow
I let go of songs of sorrow

Standing in the shadow of fear
I'm so far
Standing in the arms of hope
I'm near

I'm still standing

MERRY NEW YEAR

I marvel the New Year
I marvel the Way of Your Divine Companionship

The way my soul gets lost in your love, sweet Spirit

I marvel the New Year
I marvel at a new journey of living moment to moment in Your
Divine Presence

Have I fully surrendered myself?
I welcome the adventure of finding myself through losing
myself in You

Do I always think of You, talk story with You, love You, rest in
You?

I do, I joy in You, I look at You,
...A look of Love
Your Presence is the home of Love

I marvel the Way of Your Divine Companionship
The way You talk story with me

I marvel the New Year
Merry New Year!

ALONE IN ROME

I whispered...
Let me kiss away your tears
Let me free you from your fears
Let me be your hero
I want to see you bubble over with joy

She said...
But, oh No!
Let me cry
I've come to know when tears come,
Angels come
Everything that seems to kill me makes me feel alive
I won't live in my ever present past

Life's bumps won't slow me down
They increase my speed
I must trust to the end
I must keep going even when I cannot see

It's not about deserving and earning
It's about believing and receiving

See that only love tells
Only what is done in love will last
See how a smile or a word of love goes winged to the very end

I whispered...
Your strength gives me wings
I will see you in my dreams

Robert Uhene Maikai, Editor

James Andrade - Better ways, weather and wealth! Never forget that people can give more than they think with extra effort.

"ON THE OTHER SIDE OF THE STREET" - Dedicated to my Ohana (Family) with all love and cheerful ways

THAT IS ALL - Dedicated to my lovely, cherished wife, our kids and the rest of our *Ohana* (extended family)

NIGHT IS COMIN' - Dedicated, again, to my lovely , cherished wife, our kids and the rest of our *Ohana*

"ON THE OTHER SIDE OF THE STREET"

For many years I ran with the crowds
On the other side of the street.
I followed along with eyes closed tight
Pretended not to see.
It took a heavy hand to make me open my eyes
And see for how long I had gone
With the flow.
Then healing and wisdom were gifted me!
Healing and wisdom (!)
Ever since that day
On the other side of the street.
After leaving,
I never looked back
At the other side of the street.
For, if I had,
I might want to be there too
Just for a moment
Just long enough to abandon
For just a moment
The peace and joy,
For...What?
What did I think I had
On the other side of the street?
Health is here, sickness there

On the other side of the street.
Contentment is here,
Folly there
On the other side of the street.
Hope is here,
Despair is there
On the other side of the street.
Joy is here,
Sorrow there
On the other side of the street.
Love is here,
While hate alone waits
On the other side of the street!

THAT IS ALL

When I was a child my mother called to me,
"Son, a storm is now approaching."
But still I saw the sun.
I chose not to hear her,
I continued playing.

I was just too busy
Having so much fun,
And the sky darkened
And the rain began to fall
I ignored it.

Thunder and lightning
Forced me to recall my mother's words
So I went home
And started to cry in her open arms
Till she forgave me.

From the first moment I can recall,
Whenever I was called
I felt filled with shame
And would pretend not to hear,
Running on, living my life my way.

I didn't want to change.

But when I realized she would never forsake or abandon me,
Nor take away my choice,
I finally, saw he truth, and listened.
That is all!

NIGHT TIME IS COMIN'

Night time is comin',
the darkness oh so near.
I keep waiting for doubt and fear to disappear.
But night time is comin',
The light is disappearin'
We're waitin'
for doubt and fear to disappear.

The neighbor's poured his oil,
Lit his lamp for light.
He's gonna stay awake all night.
He brought more oil
To keep the household bright.
He says the answer
To doubt and fear will appear tonight !

I think my neighbor's such a fool
to think tonight's the night or day,
That liberty will come this way!
He should have played it cool
And saved his hard earned pay.
He shouldn't waste the time
To fast and pray.

My neighbor says he knows,

If prepared to run the race
All doubt and fear will disappear
From his place.
But surely he must also know,
There's never been a trace
Of that great promise he calls grace.

Last night the answer
Came by.
It took my neighbor to the sky.
I let my lamp go dim,
I couldn't stay awake for him,
And I never saw the answer,
Now I'm left to wonder why.

Robert Uhene Maikai, Editor

Dorothy Winslow Wright is a multi-award-winning, internationally published author and poet. Her poetry has appeared in numerous literary anthologies and magazines, including the Atlantic Advocate where "Angel Wings" was first published. Her poems appear in Savant's 2018 and 2019 Poetry Anthologies. She is an active member of the National League of American PEN Women, Honolulu Branch, currently living in Honolulu, Hawaii, USA.

Books: THE BOOK GROUP BOOK (Chicago Review Press 1993); KINDED 2018 Savant Poetry Anthology; ENTWINED - 2019 Savant Poetry Anthology.

Journals: Blue Unicorn; Mature Living; Poet; The Formalist; Time of Singing

DESIGN

QUICKENING IN THE MIST

CHRIS AND THE PRAISE SINGERS

A GATHERING OF POETS

DESIGN

The heavens are telling the glory of God -- Psalm 19:1

Cirrus clouds glide across the sky.
Draw together like pieces of a jig-saw
puzzle. Become a seamless entity.

I see God's breath in airy clouds. See
celestial hand in shaping them -- God,
the creator of all, we mortals part of it.

Like the clouds, marriage partners mold
to one another. Create new life the way
the joining clouds create a different vision.

Clouds and people -- how easily they weave
in blended harmony, each fulfilling
God's design on earth and in the sky.

QUICKENING IN THE MIST

A cloud blankets the mountain top. Dense,
no noise, it shrouds the valley, the trees, the path
to my garden. I shiver in its cloying wetness,
this swaddling cloud in my silent universe

Like a fetus in its womb, I wonder at presence
I sense but cannot see. Are fetuses aware
of the beckoning world as I am aware of God's
calling? Do they fell barred from something beyond
their ken by forces too strong to challenge? Do they
want to? Perhaps they prefer the comfort of
their cozy nests, safe from a strange unknown.

I am awed at the power of God, who lowers clouds
to swallow all surroundings -- a power that raises
the hair on the nape of my neck in this odd miasma.

Am I like the unworldly fetus? Too content
to stretch beyond my comfort zone? Can I
expand as faith develops? Am I strong
enough to break from those whose ways
of doing things no longer bland with mine?

I look to the valley. Pine trees spear the thinning
mist. A thrush sings. A cardinal flutters.

A golden ray breaks through the paling gray --
a beam of promise caught insane and carols.

CHRIS AND THE PRAISE SINGERS

Let him step to the music that he hears,
however measured or far away. - Henry David Thoreau

Sometimes he balks at coming.
Sits stubbornly in the car as if afraid
of the outside world, while Alice,
his wife, pleads with him to join us.

She has no luck until he hears the
singing on the church lanai. His
shoulders ease, and he reaches for
Alice's hand. Walks along beside her.

His tenor voice is sweet, and his eyes
light up when we sing the songs
he learned before the Alzheimer haze
flew in. He taps his foot and sings,
each word correct, each note on pitch.

When sunset dims to gray, we say
a prayer, hoping Chris will sleep
the night, yet doubting it. He sleeps
in snatches. Tosses restlessly -- but,
for a while, he found sweet peace in music.

A GATHERING OF POETS

The rhythmic sound of waves wash
on the cool Pacific shore -- music
that weaves with the creative thoughts

spilling from the inky fingers of
poets, young and old, male and female
their differences enriching texture

of the afternoon. The older sprawl
in chairs, the younger on the floor.
One pretzels into mischief shape,

her clipped short hair a piquant touch.
Backs bent, pens scrawl with speed of wind.
Do scribbled words capture salty moment?
Someone speaks, and the flow of thoughts
bends to new direction like fledgling
stream branching off from flowing river.

A gull cries. Waves crash on shore, but
the poets no longer notice. The sounds are
now a part of them and the poems they create.

Skyla Reyes - Holding on to the strength which will help us live much more essentially. Moment of discovery when do discover the moment

UNIFIED - Dedicated to my Grandma, Mary

CELEBRATE - Dedicated to my Grandma, Mary

UNIFIED

Be UNIFIED
Let us all share
The love to be UNIFIED

Whatever it is, whatever it takes
Let us grab one another's hands
And hold onto the feeling
That brings out the strength of UNITY

No memcries lost in our hearts
Not with the strength of unity
For all are becoming
Or eventually will become UNIFIED

Look back and stare at what humans see as ruin
Make it a valuable lesson
Rightly let what so many have experienced
Prevail and win triumphantly.

Be UNIFIED
Let us struggle in gladness
And bringing forth the strength from being UNIFIED

CELEBRATE

Go out and celebrate
Do it now
Call upon your inner joy
Go out and celebrate!

Don't worry if your feet are touching the ground
Of planet earth .
Live with joyful life altogether
Lift your joy and give it existence

Just go out and celebrate
Do so with playful happiness
Realize how valuable your life is
Celebrate your very existence

Celebrate your freedom
Just to be, to be, to be!
Go out and celebrate
Blast out of all your bounds and lift up your voice

Rise in blissflu celebration
Go out and zealously celebrate
That you can celebrate
Realizing that there's no time to wasted

Go out and celebrate

Do it now

Call upon your inner joy

Sing, dance and celebrate!

From the age of ten, **Karen T. Sisler** wanted to write. The opportunity came 40 years later as a general writer for the Mendota Reporter, then a short term stringer for Rockford Morning Star with several of her letters appearing in various newspapers. She won top state awards for three years running from the Mendota Federated Women's Club. Several articles in Hawaii's AAA Magazine, then Generations Magazine, and now the in-house newsletter for Hawaii Kai Retirement Community. Last year she had three poems to appear in ENTWINED - 2019 Savant Poetry Anthology.

CONSIDER THIS...

HENRY AND HIS CAT

TROPICAL DELIGHT

STORYTELLER

TWO HAIKUS

CONSIDER THIS...

Mumbling about isolation?

Consider this:

When did you last take a moment to reflect

And say to someone

"What are you reading, singing, creating?"

When did you last ask someone

"Is there something you need?"

Then listened.

When did you last tell someone

"Look out your window,"

And wave to them as if saying, "Let me give you a smile to brighten your day!"

When did you last think about helping others?

Food banks everywhere desperately need contributions.

When did you last comfort someone?

Many today are depressed and desperate

For the sound of a human voice.

When did you last tell yourself

I am one, only one

But I can lift my spirit and that of that of others.

Consider how you will spend this time...

HENRY AND HIS CAT

There was a man who lived all alone
His wife was gone, his children grown,

Upon his porch, he used to sit
Looking and listening while his wife knit.

He needed a friend with a furry coat
One to talk with as he gave it a stroke.

He went to a shelter to find a pet
There on a shelf a cat he met.

Don't want a kitten, an older one's fine
Who'll sit in my lap in the warm sunshine.

A marmalade cat with large amber eyes
Blinked as she said, "Please give me a try."

She sat upright in the front of the car
"Where's our home?" she purred. He said, "Not far."

"here's a basket in which you can rest,
or you can lie purring upon my chest.

While stretching, she asked the old man
"Is this my food; meat from a can?"

"Just a little; you go catch a mouse,

I'll sit-in on the porch in front of the house."

Two mice she laid at his feet where he sat
Where upon he whispered, "You're a really great cat!"

Henry and his cat sat warmed in the sun
Planning their future that now had begun.

TROPICAL DELIGHT

Walk along the beach at night.
See the many stars.
Reach for your lover's hand
and be whomever you are.

Feeling the cooling sand
beneath their tireless feet;
the couple sinks to the ground
letting two bodies meet.

From each other's touch
they let their senses quiver.
Rolling with rising passion,
then exhausted feel a shiver.

Slowly they arise, and walk
into the sapphire sea.
Warm waves the only witness
of my true love and me.

STORYTELLER

Tell me with your voice and words
    stories that I've not yet heard.

Tell of plants and silly birds
    and of stories that you've heard.

Tell of ocean currents deep
    and of warriors who now sleep.

Tell of peoples from afar
    who navigated here by stars.

Tell me of exotic lands
    and dragon tales from Japan

Tell of foes with planes and guns
    who made the people hide and run.

Tell of storms and huge, high waves
    that took so many to their graves.

Tell of threads and special art
    lying deep within your heart.

Storyteller, you cast a spell
   with the stories that you tell!

TWO HAIKUS

Childhood

Girls, boys laughing
jumping, running in sunlight
youth free and happy.

Rainy Day

Gray clouds dripping rain
streets slick and glistening wet
bright ponchos appear

Chinese poet-philosopher **Hongri Yuan** has had his works published in the UK, USA, India, Mexico, New Zealand, Canada and Nigeria, as well in KINDRED - 2081 Savant Poetry Anthology. The theme of his works is the exploration of human prehistoric and future civilizations. "Golden Giant" is an epic poem; its content is meant to be true, not imaginary. In it, he was inspired to explain a complex and diverse future. The worlds it depicts, such as "Platinum City," "The City of God" and so on, all came from another space-time. Everything is made up of time, everything is elapsing. Outside this world, there is another world, invisible, with a higher civilization that will eventually come into this world. The work was translated into English by Yuanbing Zhang

THE GOLEDEN GIANT

GOLEDEN GIANT

Who is sitting in the heavens and staring at me?
Who is sitting in the golden palace of tomorrow?
Who is smiling?
Golden staff in his hand
flashes a dazzling light.
Ah, the flashes of lightning-
interweave over my head...
I walked into the crystalline corridor of the time-
I want to open
the doors of gold.
Lines of words in the sun-
Singing to me in the sky-
I want to find
the volumes of gold poems
on the shores of the new century
to build the city of gold.

Laozi with rosy cheek and white hair-
Smiles at me in the clouds,
A phoenix dances trippingly
and carries with it, a book of gold.

Lines of mysterious words
made my eyes drunken,

countless giant figures
came towards me from the clouds.

Ages through seventy million years
emerged leisurely before my eyes,
the cities of gold
surrounded with crystalline gardens.

A sky of sapphire
sent out a colorful miraculous brightness,
onto green hills of jasper,
dragons and phoenixes were flying

Exquisite pagoda-
with majestical palace of gold,
the airy pavilions and pagodas
stood within the purple-red clouds

Laughing girls
riding the colorful husbands and wives,
propitious clouds
sprinkling the colorful flowers.

I opened the door to a golden palace,
saw the rows of scrolls of gold,
a giant who had the haloes all over his body-
there was a golden sun over his head.

Smiling, he picked up the books of gold
recited the sacred verses-
Intoxicated with the miraculous wonderful words
I was enveloped with purple-gold flames.

A golden lotus
bloomed beneath my feet,
lifted up my body,
wafting it up out of the golden palace

The red clouds
drifted by my side,
in the far distance I saw
another golden paradise

the leisurely bells
calling to me.
There- countless giants
roamed in a golden garden,

with skies of ruby,
rounds of sun
like the golden lotus
blooming in the sky,

intoxicating fragrances of flowers
like sweet good wine,

golden trees
laden with the dazzling diamonds,

wonderful flowers
in bloom for a thousand years,
this land of gold
inlaid with the gems.

The pavilions of gold were
strewn at random, clustered in multitude.
Someone was playing chess
Someone was chatting...

Quaint clothes
colossal statures
miraculous eyes-
happy and comfortable.

White cranes
flying in the sky,
husbands and wives
crowing leisurely.

Beside an old man I approached
as if he were waiting for me
in this golden pavilion.
He opened an ancient sword casket-

A glittering ancient sword
engraved with abstruse words and expressions,
which were clear and transparent, like lightning,
dimly glowed with purplish-red patterns.

He told me a metaphysical epic:
The sword came from nine billions years ago,
made from hundreds of millions of suns.
It was a sacred sword of the sun-

It could pierce the rocks of time,
open layer after layer of skies,
let the sacred fires forge the heaven and the earth
into golden paradises.

The old man's eyes were deep, archaic, difficult to discern-
Dimly showing the joyful flames.
He let me take this sword
to fly towards a new golden paradise:

The huge golden lotus floated leisurely-
I flew among the skies, for a thousand miles.
Huge pyramids
loomed impressively in front of my eyes

Mountainous figures of giants
walked about in front of the pyramid,

the huge pyramids of gold
far taller than the mountains.

The giant trees of gold
like a forest
stood in the sky
laden with the stars.

The multi-colored propitious clouds
were like a colossal bird
in a silvery sky,
crowing joyfully.

I came to the front of a pyramid-
a door was opening wide for me,
a group of blond giants
sat with smiles in the grand palace.

An old and great holy man
recited in monotone.
The temple was painted with the magical symbols
and giant portraits of Gods.

The palace was full of silvery white light
blooming with magnificent flowers,
a peal of wonderful mellifluous bells
that made one suddenly forget all time.

I heard an immemorial verse
that was written hundreds of millions of years past,
relating countless eras of giants,
the creation of the holy kingdoms of heaven.

Their wisdom was sacred and great
knowing, omnisciently, the past and the future of the universe.
They flew freely among the skies
landed on the millions of planets in the universe.

They altered time per one's pleasure,
encompassed other powers, such as-
turning stone into gold,
making gold bloom into flowers.

They were like the bulbous sun,
which could erupt with sacred flames
let all things blaze in raging flames..
Manifest imagination into reality..

They landed on planets
establishing golden paradises
and with their magical, cryptic wisdom
built platinum cities.

I saw the splendid words
spied from the volume of gold

and the magical wonderful halos
rotating like colorful lightning in the sky.

I came to another wonderful planet,
saw a massive monumental edifice of platinum,
the whole city, an intricate work of art
emanating, softly, a brilliant white light.

A huge round square
encased unearthly works.
Giants of great stature
came and went leisurely in the street.

They wore spartan, common clothing
covering their bodies,
all with smiles upon their faces,
both men and women looked beautiful.

They spoke a wonderful language
intriguing and pleasant as welcome music.
Some of them travelled by spaceship
flying around silently in the sky.

I walked into a towering edifice of platinum-
saw a magnificent hall,
its platinum walls were inlaid with gems,
among which was a row of unusual instruments.

Their eyes were like bright springs
and they wore multi-colored clothes.
Some were operating the instruments.
Some were talking softly among themselves.

I saw a fascinating picture, a simulacrum that
drew giant planets,
arranged cities on those planets,
with crystal gardens.

I opened a crystal door-
noticed a group of men and women, who were happily,
singing softly,
with glittering books of gold in their hands.

Arrangements of flowers and glasses filled of golden wine
sat on the huge round table.
Golden walls were sparkling
carved with all kinds of wonderful images.

I saw a demure girl,
with sparkling golden halo above her head,
adorned in a lengthy purple-gold dress
peerless in its quality.

Pages- were marked with cryptic glyphs
or lines of ancient magic words or symbols,

each of their books were made of gold
inexplicably constructed in golden crystal.

I understood their euphonious songs-
They were singing the sacred love
They were singing great ancestors
They were recounting the civilization of the universe

Gardens filled their city, everywhere,
surrounded with the sweet rivers.
The whole earth was a piece of jade,
the clay, a translucent layer of golden sands.

I saw enormous bright, white spheres
suspended high above the city,
emanating outwards a dazzling light-
illuminating the skies and earth- bright as the crystal

The towering, great buildings stood in great numbers
As if carved by a singular piece of platinum.
Doves and colorful birds
were flying among the heavens.

A mono-train was
flying swiftly through the sky,
the streets were illuminated in bright white,
and any moving vehicle could not have been seen.

These people's bodies were unusually strong.
Playing a wonderful game-
they piled up the pieces of great stones
arranging into grotesque works.

Similar to giant eyes
and ancient totems,
there were strange birds
covered with lightning feathers.

I saw a couple of tall lovers-
aviators, riding in their spaceship.
Their eyes were quiet and bright,
colorful halo around their bodies.

This wonderful space was gyrating leisurely
like a huge, resplendent crystal.
I said goodbye to the unusual city,
towards a space of golden light.

The cities flashed in the sky.
I flew over the layers of the sky again
and I saw a new-fangled world:
the multi-colored city of crystal.

The high towers were exquisitely carved
displaying multi-colored pearls,

layers of its eave painted with dragon and phoenix,
hung with singing golden bells.

The earth was a crystal garden,
the palaces were limpid and crystal,
huge mountains were like a transparent gems
lined with the golden trees.

I saw the tall giants-
who wore their purple clothes,
with heads of round suns,
bodies enshrined with halos.

They sat up in the main halls
singing a mellifluous song.
Some were roaming leisurely in the garden.
Some were summoning the birds in the sky.

The crystalline airy pavilions and pagodas
were beset with jewels and agates,
a huge jewel on the spire,
shining golden lights.

I saw a holy giant
sitting in the middle of a main hall
the purple-gold flame, flashed around his body,
which filled with the whole majestic main hall.

Full-bodied fragrance filled the hall
like a cup of refreshing wine.
Solemn expression was merciful and joyful,
a huge book was in his hand.

The hall was full of men and women
listening quietly to the psalms of the saints,
the lotuses were floating in the sky
where the smiling giants sat.

The golden light poured down from the sky
bathing the whole of this crystal kingdom.
The jewels above the giant towers-
the golden suns.

The golden walls of a golden tower
were carved with the lines of golden words I had glimpsed-
hovering around the dragons and phoenixes,
as if they were intonating the inspiring poems.

The smiling giants in the sky-
With wide halo flashing around their bodies,
were each dignified and tranquil,
floating in the golden translucent sky.

I flew over this crystal kingdom,
saw a vast golden mountain in the distance

sending out the brilliant lights in the sky
where the propitious clouds were blossoming.

This was a golden giant
sitting in the golden translucent sky
his body composed of thousands of millions of constellations
the golden sun rotating on his forehead.

He lit up the whole marvellous universe-
the kingdoms of heaven shone in the sky.
Here there was no the sky nor earth,
lights of pure gold emanated in every direction.

The smiling giants were sitting
on the gold-engraved pavilions.
The pavilions levitated in the translucent sky
shining the layers of purple-gold light.

A scene of multi-colored translucent mountains,
propitious clouds floating in the heavens,
large wonderful flowers blooming in the mountain peaks,
trees of pure light.

A river flowed from the sky
and with river bottom reflecting a layer of golden sand.
There were strange and beautiful birds and beasts
some like aerial phantoms.

This was a world of light.
Everything was made of light.
The divine light formed all things
and the golden paradises.

The golden giant-
shines the kingdoms of heaven within his body.
The cities of gold-
brilliant and fascinating in his bones.

I observed lines, words of incredible profundity
arranged into a huge book in the sky.
It seemed as if they were the bright stars
constituting a wonderous drawing.

There was a golden pavilion in the sky
guarded with behemoth dragons and phoenixes.
An old man with a whisk
waved to me and smiled in the pavilion,

I seem to be attracted by some sort of magic-
leisurely came to his side.
He told me the golden giant
was namely my great ancestor

This was an eternal palace-
There's no concept of time here.

Holy light- was exactly the God.
What I witnessed was better than the heavens.

He pointed to the huge book in the sky
told me that it was the mystery of the universe.
The book contained magical wisdom,
created the countless worlds of gold.

He pointed to a pagoda in the sky,
told me that it was the temple of words.
The light turned into the sacred words,
and the words created the time of gold.

He held up a very large pearl
in which flashed the pictures (and all images).
He told me that it was the future time-
the embodiment of all the wonderful worlds.

He told me that it was another universe.
Still desiring to go to these paradises,
he gave me the magical pearl,
to let it be my future guide.

I said goodbye to the old holy man,
set afoot onto a new road towards the heavens again.
I sat in a golden pavilion-
lightly flew to the distant outer space...

Robert Uhene Maikai, Editor

Daniel S. Janik is a physician, educator, environmentalist, linguist, author, poet, photographer and videographer with over seventy published works across numerous genres using a variety of pen names. Single-author poetry book publications include FOOTPRINTS, SMILES AND LITTLE WHITE LIES (Savant 2008), THE ILLUSTRATED MIDDLE EARTH (Savant 2008), and LAST AND FINAL HARVEST (Savant 2008). Contributing poet to the last ten years of Savant Poetry Anthology series and Editor for FIFTY-EIGHT STONES (Savant 2012) and BELLWETHER MESSAGES (Savant 2013). He has authored two children's books, A WHALE'S TALE (Savant 2008), and THE TURTLE DANCES (Savant 2013). His educational book, UNLOCK THE GENIUS WITHIN (Rowman and Littlefield Education 2005) remains a pioneering work. "Clean Water, Common Ground" (Savant Media/K. Simmons Productions 2020), his documentary on the state of the earth's fresh water received two Telly awards for best documentary.

FUGUE IN D FOR NIGHTWATCHERS

CROSSBORDERS

THINGS LEFT UNDONE

FUGUE IN D FOR NIGHTWATCHERS

Did you water the grass today
Like I asked you?
Yes, Pa.
Did you take out the trash?
Yes, Pa.
Did you lock all the doors?
Just like you asked, Pa.
Did you...?
Yes, Pa.
An' the car's washed and waxed,
An' the air cooler's turned on,
An' the stove fire is cold,
All like you want, Pa.
Ready for night.
All's closed up 'sept this window here
Just by my bed.
I like to look out at the night sky
An' feel the night wind
Gently caress my body.
I like to leave one window open
For Night to come in.
She's all I got.
Goodnight then, Kid.
Goodnight, Pa.

CROSSBORDERS

Kilo, Kilo!
Across the border
They come in kilos
The dust, the grit, the aching days upon each back
Looking towards the Northern Gods

Kilo, Kilo!
They cry like curling buzzards,
Greedily eyeing the living dead
Slaves of the very gods they look to
Carrying kilos of lost obsessions—
joy, hope, peace—

Kilo, Kilo!
In kilos they come
Migrating wherever the walls
Seem less stalwart
Looking for more fertile mating grounds.

THINGS LEFT UNDONE

There are things left undone
Beneath a warm sun
You will lose all you have
If you do that
They say.

So each sultry day
I try a new way
Uncharted, unknown,
Isolated, alone,
Searching for that which eludes me

Sailing inside
On a changeable tide
Towards an unseen horizon,
I dive in blind
And wait to discover whatever I find

I go with the tide
(whichever abides)
When the moment seems right
Neither here nor away
And end up with nowhere and nothing to say

I look far afar

Aloha La'a Kea -- Sacred Light of Love

Without sun or a star
To glimpse where we are
Without leaving a scar
With never a promise to guide by.

Robert Uhene Maikai, Editor

Rüdiger Herzing Rückmann has written poetry most of his life and studied under the guidance of poets Tess Gallagher and Hayden Carruth. He is Director of Advancement at Pacific Buddhist Academy where he also teaches poetry and German. He is the author of "Offering" in *Friends Journal* and has had poems shown in exhibits and galleries, including the Albright-Knox Art Gallery in Buffalo, New York.

THE BALLAD OF AMELIA EARHART

FILET MIGNON

INDIGO

LANGUAGE OF THE HOUSE OF SPARROWS

THE BALLAD OF AMELIA EARHART

All I wanted was to fly higher,
to find endless skies.

Men determined too much of my life:
a father, giddy from flights of wine
who came crashing down
from his career and then we had to leave
one town after another until I found
more promising horizons and offers
to soar into the unknown.

But why did fame always greet me
with men who wanted marriage
to keep me safe and home?

I had to prove them wrong,
to fly higher and solo,
to hold my own and not drown
if I came too close to the sun.

All along, though, I knew
someday I would come down
so far that I would never
again leave the ground,
and men who ground me forever

except when they decide to tease me
about my one last flight
as if perhaps I'm still around
like a myth who never leaves
with wings intact or broken,
whose final act is interrupted,
tragic and unspoken.

FILET MIGNON

Autumn in Stratford, Ontario,
after the Shakespeare Festival
my sister joined her classmates
for dinner, already sated with the finest
poetry that our mother, a high school
English teacher, ordered for her daughter
on an evening lined in gold and crimson leaves
that fall early in Canada.

The filet mignon my sister chose at the restaurant
was overcooked, a bit gristly, served hurriedly
by staff thick into their evening shifts,
not knowing the high school girls
already were certain of their tastes
long before they would cut through the world
as teachers, doctors, attorneys, mothers,
some as betrayed wives on the rebound

who years later might take their own children
up north to whet their appetite for life
and all that is good and right
even if meals don't live up to their billing,
to learn that filet mignon can be savored
if cut in small portions, exposed to heat

but not dried out, enhanced with gentle sauce,
so it will more likely keep its flavor.

INDIGO

Every day I wondered if my indigo might fade
in fifty years, if someone would match my blue
from leaves I bundled and removed from water
fermented and beaten with lime. Every day I ripened
with that hard paste before all was ready for dyeing.

Will anyone wonder how I stayed true to the only life
I knew for years in a tired sun, my bones heavy as stone?
I had no choice, only hope for my children to love me
for making a shade of blue to keep them safe in a sparse home,
a royal hue for the rich who stayed blind to my stained hands.

LANGUAGE OF THE HOUSE SPARROWS

House sparrows find my open office
in Oahu every day. They enter curious
or hungry and stay only moments,
enough to alight on familiar ground
but rarely far from easy flight.

One evening my father died. Distant
and growing weaker, he lost his voice.
Soon his soul escaped for a sea of Light.
A house sparrow, insistent,
stayed near me and then I knew.

The next day my sister called
to share what the sparrow
had already proclaimed,
and grief surged in me like small waves
that always return like the birds who visit
their language familiar, determined, and brief.

Robert Uhene Maikai, Editor

93

Born and raised in Tupika , Kansas, **Chuck St. Louis** graduated from University of Hawaii with a Masters degree and works as a hospital administer, living life in abundance and letting a special one walk alongside. An avid sports-fan, he asks, "How about those Kansas Chiefs -- amazingly well-done." It's all about love supreme on a one-on-one level in a personal way.

IAN THE MAN THOR - dedicated to my gorgeous wife and the entire family.

JUST YOU AND ME, HOW SPECIAL - dedicated to the love of my life, my partner and treasured wife and the entire family

HEAD CRACKING - Like the old saying, "Its time to have a cold one..." - dedicated to my lovingly supportive partner, my tender gracious wife, and the entire extended family far and wide.

IAN THE MAN THOR

Oh, the blessings up above the stars and heavens
In the numerous multitude of lights above
For thus, may the one
Designed by a caring other
Glow brightly, radiant in the heart.

Further how its time,
Moment now to be carefully,
Overwhelmingly loved by a treasure of delight from above!

Do let the Spirit of Love be bonded in peace with much joy to
Perpetuate the lasting love
To be shared thanks to a special one.

By all intent
Gladly be lifted
In heart to things above
With much giving of the gift of Love!

JUST YOU AND ME, HOW SPECIAL

So can't be without you,
You are all and everything.
Just never imagineD how special
You could come to be to me.

For being two lost shells
stuck in on the shore sand
Washed up holding
each others hands.

As each our hearts beat together
Upon the shoreline sun rays
No can't be without you, dear,
Being totally my all and everything.

No, just never ever imagine
How special it could tremendously be
As do take heart away and know
About the love wanting to live for .

And nothing in this entire world
Can ever separate us
Or our forever lasting endearment
Our devotion and loyalty for one

Forevermore

Memorable loving
Forevermore
Can't be without you.

HEAD CRACKING

Go crackling when crack the bottle on the head
Look ahead as will keep the laughter well-fed
Now crack the bottle on the head.

No its not infatuation
To know 'bout what did happen.
But it's time in coming
To realize time will take a halt.

Do caution to crack the bottle on head
For may regret it ever
'Specially if spilling an ounce or two.

Adrenaline will make it seem
Like merry-go-round
Swirling as whirls keep on
Never seeming to stop turning.

Go crack the bottle on the head
So laughing and smiling
But knowing will be waking up

Next morning
With a compound aching agonizing Headache
Asking the simple, down to Earth question,
"Was it all really so much worth it?"

Robert Uhene Maikai, Editor

Michael Lau - Love is always evident, if sought.

ALIKA - dedicated to my family, church, and my beautiful partner and wife.

GO PLEAD - dedicated to my family, church, and my beautiful partner and wife.

ALIKA

Alika, Alika, Alika,
Faster than lightning
Above the stars shining
A light.
So thus
All know Alika.

Alika, Alika, Alika
Opens the heart to share
With all delight.
A channel,
A pathway
To the pure
Llight residing
Around and above .

Alika, Alika, Alika
Carries the glowing torch
For so many
To see
The radiant warmth
Reflecting light
Leading to the steps
To Heaven's gateway

Heaven's majestic beauty.

Alika, Alika, Alika
Sending out the message
For all those observing
But not experiencing
The glory
Of the vastness
In which
Living a life
Lost in not knowing
But still comprehend ing
the love , love , love
Abundantly abounding in
Alika, Alika, Alika!

GO PLEAD

Go plead
For an offering
Go plead
Together
Forever

Go plead
For that which makes all
Sufficient
Then present it to the heart in making,
A conclusive choice
For the satisfaction of living.

Go plead
Now to open the heart
Of all
Everyone
in every way
Unconditionally
Go plead
For love
Deserved
But yet unfound.

Milionea Toluao - Rejoice for better life

THE FIRST OF ALL - dedicated to my precious son

EVER MUCH KINDNESS, EXALTED - dedicated to my precious son

MY PLACE TAKEN - dedicated to my precious son

THE FIRST OF ALL

Bliss
The First of All
Comfort
Goodness
Kindness

Caring
The First of All
Sincerity
Love
Joy

Gladness
The First of All
Elevated
Levitated
Lifted up

Power
The First of All
Majesty
Glory
Presence, Here and Now

EVER MUCH KINDNESS, EXALTED

I turning over everything
For love and comfort
Exclusively from ever much kindness, exalted.

Above evermore
I seek gratitude
Gratitude for ever much kindness

I give thanks in appreciation
With sincere love
For a haven in ever more kindness

I pour out of own self
All my goodness
Seeking a way to ever much kindness

I light a candlestick lamp
It glows with power
Lighting my path to ever much kindness

I reach out and shine
Sacrificial love
Hoping to gain ever much kindness

I triumph in victory
Over torment and decay
Having attained ever much kindness, exalted

Robert Uhene Maikai, Editor

MY PLACE TAKEN

Shame
Blame
Pain and humiliation

Condemnation
Wrath
Upon the creation.

Hope
Death
Gasp for the soul

Bare
Acceptance
Transformation of meaning

Love
Rescue
Refuge forevermore

Christopher Scott Halicion - Keeping the heart always freshly in love

A PLACE HOLY - dedicated to my loving *ohana* daughter Elizabella and son Jason.

LOVE IS EVER SPLENDID - dedicated to my loving ohana daughter Elizabella and son Jason.

A PLACE HOLY

Supplication,
Consecration...
The holy place.

Attestation
Castigation...
The holy place.

Animation
Celebration...
The holy place.

Circumspection
Contemplation...
A place holy.

LOVE IS EVER SPLENDID

In the valley of luster of green
Bewildered by contention
On a rock of love
Doing the act
Hearts heaving
Back and forth
In reasonable desire for one another.

Lost in time
Which has dramatically
Stopped
In their act
Of love and desire.
How does brutality
Open up to feel true desire and love?

Not giving way to anything
Outside the valley
The sounds embellishing
The act are kept
In the corridors
Of the valley of narrowing mountains
Shape mystically...

Robert Uhene Maikai, Editor

Brent Kutara - Being one who lets go and lets God...

BECAUSE - dedicated to the one special person making a way ready to be together.

"DO YOUR...THING" - dedicated to the one special person making a way ready to be together.

BECAUSE

Wonderful is glory in glory
Given unquestionably each every day
Because
Of all
In hope
In affectation
In precious living
Day-to-day
The precious gift of life.

Wonderful is solace in solace
A blessing to all
Because
In the tender abode
In peace
In joy
hour-to-hour
The gratitude of the heart

Wonderful is knowing the knowable
A kind of love sacrifice
Because
In the sharing

In the awakening
In thankfulness most endearing
Second-to-second
Pure love is given

It is so
Because of you,
Dearest one,.
Because of you.

"DO YOUR...THING"

Do your...Thing
Live life
In grief, hope, joy or anger
But do it with faith, knowing
That behind the making of all things
Is a heart love.

Do all the...Things
That make life what it is
struggle, expectation, fun or acerbic
But always do it with belief
That within all things
Is a single, ever-present soul of compassion

Multi-award-winning poet, **Uhene (Robert Maika'i Jr)**, lives in the beautiful, paradise state of Hawaii. Single, no children, he loves people and anything that tastes of the mango. His Grandfather, Kawika Smith from Molokai, took him to first theater movie at five years of age, a Samurai production, and thus began his poetic career on the streets of Waikiki.

Uhene's poems appear in BELLWETHER MESSAGES - 2013 Savant Poetry Anthology; RUNNING FROM THE PACK - 2015/16 Savant Poetry Anthology, SHADOW AND LIGHT - 2017 Savant Poetry Anthology and KINDRED - 2018 Savant Poetry Anthology. He is the guest editor for this year's Savant poetry anthology.

MONICA - dedicated to the class of 1991 at Master's University

COME FORTH BEAUTY - dedicated to Bill and Karen Harper

ONE SOLIDARITY OF TONE - dedicated to my three nephews and two nieces

SO IT'S NOW - dedicated to Praise Chapel Witmore, Wahiawa Pastor Steve and Earl

SWEET FRAGRANCE OF LOVE VALUABLE TREASURE - dedicated to Pastor Keven Akana

MONICA

Lasting forevermore love being yours,
Do expand far up,
Up above to find
Your shining special one!

Do let the stars of Heaven
Brighten your pathway,
Even as love initiates your journey
Following your heart, most dear one!

May you continually carry the spirit of gentle Aloha-love,
Exposing all beauty
To those who yearn
Like you.

Further explore the depths
The clarity of hearts,
The sharing of imminent chords of harmonies
And abandon yourself
To lasting forevermore love.

COME FORTH BEAUTY

Do shower down the blessings with radiant light,
Glowing immaculately to shoot back home
The power of the magnificent,
Being loved -- all encompassed -- in great satisfaction.

Rise, Rise, Rise
Come forth out of void
Hold no sin.
Let death remain in the grave.

Rise, Rise, Rise
Come forth out of void
Hold no sin.
Let death keep in the grave.

Shower down the blessings with glowing immaculate light,
Shine forth with the power of magnificent love,
Encompassing all in the greatest satisfaction.

RISE, RISE, RISE, COME FORTH!

ONE SOLIDARITY OF TONE

So what beauty do so see! Do what manner so see such beauty?
What causes to take notice of such a spectacular figure of
crystal clear
refreshment so very hard to put together the mystery.

What known manner does allow taking part of lovely
elegance of beauty! Which tickles own observation of it. Do
let's so
have a heart expanding upwards to ultimate Creator, to view
the
vastness of it all. Stop now, and try to understand what is said
on a
holistic way of thought and neither provoking clue cognitive
patterns
of manner.

Your beauty produced for compassionate people worth
knowing the depth and width of moments. It's how a new
direction
of angelic celestial bells ringing above high to one solidarity of
tone.
How your beauty being in one discretely and soberly
configuration

This ready to get serious to drop down to one knee, for its
intensely
on living in such a pleasant condition .

So by allowing others to benefit eternally in having
awestruck lights shining, giving honor reflectively on
livelihood.
Go only love! Delicately just waiting for that one true love.
Now
with the shaping beauty, an enormous capacity for told .

No mourners here. No not just right here among an array
of brilliant lightning stars for not only those high above the
skies.
But those who are close right near before my eyes. So totally
devoted to tell own heart to burn with engulfed desires. No one
else but just sweet devotion . Which having the capacity to
change
a heart in the betterment of an honorable life.

Do let the rightful dominance making all that could truly be
without nothing being compared to your fragrances of the
reality of
beauty. So has my heart been overtaken at all measures,
absolutely
just a certified love. As the inner light shines to dedicate

existing presence being desired totally. Suddenly an anchor of love in being the only way to go full blast in all everything, on every level or just not at all-. Do understand the very deep implications. The life to live the best today and leave everything
on the table. Because realizing tomorrow is not promised at all.

It's a lot better to be safe than painfully sorry. Do less stress , just press forward in process! So coming back to heart, never been a love like this ever. Do keep in mind striving in being
best in any amount of energy amused in all possibilities. Don't want to never assume. Declare by a lifelong full of how's the world is perceived wholeheartedly obtained. But the effort done
was the very best given in all heart, in not holding back to no one.

But why ask so many questions? Do really viewed ready to get serious visit. And is it laid upon heart? Then so need to see
it through going all in the end to complete what purpose put on the
planet. Notwithstanding, be the hero too sometimes . But don't plan on taking the last shot. So let's have the joy the angels know

all about. As the gentleman over to the left is quite dashing, so wants the point to be known. How seeming to be the figure, while
others represent the past.

Freak out , ill-rationally, noratic, emotional called being F.I.N.E in exam how mood comes and goes. Do use it fondly displaying the heart of mind never vto sell soul. Now by agreeing
on something one doesn't believe such, sets foot on the winning track to success. No public announcement for appearance.
But as some logical question will give better rational answers!

Did just show up unannounced with no hindrance.
But do bring together the many intangibles molded into successful
enlightenment. Do nowto top it off with the loving grace pour over as
going down in holding on for safety reasons.

For may not be aware of a sudden stop happening.
Do ever think for a minute how would go out like an over use garbage
bag. At the moment of time to fall and fall in the occasion. Suddenly

going in getting grove on. Now just recharging batteries been 'bout
the door. Do brought the beauty of love to the whole world plain and
simple nodding of love, love, love the composite in the understanding of
the source and sustainability of resources.

SO IT'S NOW

Do need being most close to the existence of life. For only do
delightfully function and exist . By helping giving a hand upon every step of the way,
but in not having the direction in doing or trying things on the very necessities will
sooner or later deflate.

Its all to bring bare conscience in rolling over in shining , revealing
In plucking out the light in any deformities making less of what truly is adorable to
gain better and most highly be . Lets be one truly living adherently in the right manner of
life to be filled exceedingly in much strength of joyfulness

So daily in need indeed of all help in the uncomfortable sufferings
not being appeased in much about living. But just as a child with a running nose
desperate for a teacher to come and wipe it,

Do ultimately truly being God's way of love in a nose wiper,

and able to teach others to do the same. Now afterwards
sharing the healing to wipe
noses that no other or even own person can have an ability to
wipe what is needed,
Which demonstrates the heart of compassion pure love.

This is a work of a strong mind with everyone in calling for
help in
relieving pain and suffering from each one experiencing going
deep down deeper
than a knife to get out the bacteria of disease in close to death
incidents. Do find the
place of refuge carried into the arms of love to hold being most
reassured.

Now having wings to fly freely being the best in whatever
needed
with the tranquility of comfort provided by the heart of pure
love given by the ultimate
gift of grace which is all the price of love amazingly!

SWEET FRAGRANCE OF LOVE VALUABLE TREASURE

The sweet fragrance from the heavens giving the beauty
The aroma of tropical love .

Your Beauty is
    Immeasurable,
    Immeasurable,
    Immeasurable,
Just a blossoming flower with an abundant of forensic freshly
Saulter, wishfully colorful and glitter's holding up the stars in
the orbit.

As sparkling
Delightfully with the brilliance on a soberly dark glimpse in the
silent space
    Immeasurable,
    Immeasurable,
    Immeasurable,
My souls empty without your presence,
But senses come alive

Once again with the nearness , closeness being here .
Do experience in quality to qualify in proving value added
service

Immeasurable,

Immeasurable,

Immeasurable

So seem such special place overwhelmingly serene sanctuary with

Much extensive love, transmute elite class of elegance to clarity.

A deposit of the

Valuable fortified treasures .

Immeasurable,

Immeasurable,

Immeasurable,

Allows the privilege to ask for guidance in the

Awareness, Completeness and Optimalness!

Miranda Zhang - So precious, dearest love only a father can give.

DEAR FATHER - dedicated to family and friends , and to anyone who needs a helping hand

DEAR FATHER

Thanks for your unfailing love
That has shielded through time.
In my moments of brokenness
You raised me up
And called me by name.

I love you with all my heart,
And know that
You love me, too,
And know how much I love you.

I so long to hear your voice,
So sweet,
So peaceful,
So full of love.
Every time call your name
I know you will be there.

I long so for your presence
I need you for me to be stronger
In whatever tests life may hold

I would gladly give my life, my heart and soul
To have you here beside me once again
Even if just for a moment

I love you, father.
I am your daughter
In whom you delight.

Robert Uhene Maikai, Editor

131

Sidney Esperas - Sometimes,when least expecting, one finds true being in need.

NEED - dedicated to my two daughters from their loving Dad

NEED

Need, want, desire
every moment
upon every occasion
every second
each and every day

For clarity
brilliance
genuine
gratifying
a reflection of and to others

Let me shine forth magnificently
Awesome
Beautiful
Unsullied
A living comfort to all in
Need
Want and
Desire.

Paul Giovenco - There is only one True Way: A remarkable life journey gained from the vast experiences of everyday life.

THE ANSWER IS THE QUESTION - dedicated to family and friends who have helped me navigat the jungles of life

THE ANSWER IS THE QUESTION

What is the answer?
Where is it?
I may not even be passing the class
(which class?)
But I must find the answer.

Beginning to end,
I must know the answer.
A way to accomplish life's goals
(what goals?)
Certainly there is an answer! There must be!

Mustn't there?

An Avenger?
A shield and defender?
I must release despair
(what despair?)
And rescue myself
Needing only the answer.

But what is the answer
In this disturbed world?
That's the question!
(what question?)

Ah, so the answer *is* the question
The question, the answer.

Robert Uhene Maikai, Editor

137

Eddie Aribon - The greatest kindness is being set free

NO ENDLESS SIGHT - dedicated to all people around the world going through a difficult event

NO ENDLESS SIGHT

O' glorious night
no endless sight.

Being King of all,
Pure delight.

The purpose unseen
Forever preserved

The target
Belief

That heart condition
Tenderized by pounding.

The voice within
Heard at last.

Now endless sight,
No glorious night.

The debris (for there always is some)
Keeps the mind from inquiring.

Where was no way
and their is:

Endless sight

Never seen
Never night.

Robert Uhene Maikai, Editor

Chino Villa - It's for the spirit to give clarity.

REIGNING INN - dedicated to my two daughters

REIGNING INN

Reigning in
At Reigning Inn
To tugs at my elbow
I must reign in now -- today -- finally -- at last.

Reigning Inn,
I look to see if someone greater than I
Is, at last, in fact, reigning me in
Seeking to guide me finally home.

What home?
Why me?
Where will my journey home take me?
What someone-greater-than-I?

An Immaculately conceived
Keeper?
Lover? Friend?
Who is it that promises me a map to find my way home?

Someone-greater-than-me,
Are you looking to the day that I will bow head to you?
Or is it enough for me to reign in
The pride, the feelings, the fears that you're reigning in?

And what will I find at "home?"

143

Food?

Shelter? Respite?

Provide for me first, then, perhaps,

I will invite you to follow me home.

Robert Uhene Maikai, Editor

145

Cathy A. Schultz was born in Honolulu on Oahu, Hawaii. I was fortunate to experience the subcultures of the United States of America by living in five states, attending twelve schools before graduating with honors from high school. Also, I have been married for thirty-five years with two adult children and five grandchildren. Being awarded several scholarships allowed me to attend University of Hawaii at Manoa, Honolulu Community College, and a host of academic opportunities. Writing, music, and cultural anthropology fascinates me.

MAGENTA SKY - to my husband, Paul

SEEDS OF CHANGE - to my husband, Paul

WHAT DO YOU DO? - to my husband, Paul

IF - to my husband, Paul

YOU - to my husband, Paul

MAGENTA SKY

Did you hear the sunset fall?
Did you hear what the seagulls saw?
Footprints on the sand castle wall...

Oh, feel the salty breeze...
Click and clatter of palm leaves...
Wave hello and call for me.

Deep breathe in and look up high
Pink cotton-candy clouds drift by
And stick to the Sea Aura Sky.
Mark my Magenta sky Good-bye.

Oh, don't you Realize
You don't need to shade those hazel eyes?
Sinking sand beneath our feet.
Skinny dipped hour glass mannequin
Slip out of the jasper sea.

Don't ask me, "Why?"
Just breathe in and look up high
Look up high, Magenta Sky.

Swaying to the music beat.
Swaying to the rhythmic heat.
Heartfelt Love is such a Treat.

147

Dance so long, we don't feel our feet.
The Oceanic lapping.
We'll meet again laughing.

Look for me in the jasper sea.
Where Love is Forever.
Together, we'll be.

Our only alibi is our Shoes.
Swaying to the music,
Where everything is new.

SEEDS OF CHANGE

There once was a ground that lay barren and fallow
And knew not its power of the seeds planted shallow.
These seeds were carefully and lovingly placed
In the soil that was only overlooked in haste.

The promise of rain was in distant, lightening glisten.
Far off, sounds of rumbling thunder brought rain drops to
Those seeds of change. "Only Listen…"
And hear the fall of the refreshing rain,
Only to water the seeds of change.

There's a new day dawning
As the sun's rays purred warmth to that ground,
The seeds of change heard the purr pressing green blades
Toward that sunny sound.

The flittering shadows of Time-ebb and flow;
Those seeds of change began to grow.
The field of blades was a muddy mess.
To the casual observer, just weeds rippling to wind's caress.

Days and weeks and moments passed.
Those seeds of change turned to grass.
Yet, to the one with a keen, caring eye, those
Seeds of change grew into a garden with butterflies.

There were Daisies of Hope, Courage, and Love.
Swaying Ying and Yang, A balance rarely heard of.
Those daisies, they lasted much longer than most.
Year after year, there were dragon fly hosts.

The soil that once lay barren and fallow,
Found its Power in the Seeds of Change
Planted shallow.

WHAT DO YOU DO?

What do you do
When it was their spirit
That gave you such joy to your life and soul?
What do you do when you love them so?
What do you do when their closeness
Is no longer near?

What do you do
When their courage
Took away your fear?

What do you do
When those eyes that so moved you
Are now closed?

What do you do
When they loved you-just you-the very most?

You'll miss that someone so very special.
You'll wish that it just wasn't so.
You'll weep at the loss of such a good heart.
You'll wrestle and then you'll let go.
You'll know you did what they wanted
When they said,
"It's time to let me go."

IF

If you have ever felt betrayed,
Then you have known Trust.

If you have ever been down, Then you have known Joy.

If you have ever been lacking, Then you have known Plenty.

If you have ever cried tears of pain, Then you have tears of
Laughter.

If you have ever been cold,
Then you have known warmth.

If you have ever been too serious,
Then you have known how to play.

If you have ever been heart broken, Then you have known True
Love.

YOU

I would've died of a broken heart
But you mended it instead.
I would've been beneath the soil
But you placed flowers upon my head.

I would've had idle hands
But you let me hold your heart.
I would have run barefoot
Across the broken glass
But you gave me shoes to dance.
I cried upon your shoulder
About a lover in my past.

Then you dried my tears
By leading me into the sun.
You took me to see the ocean
And told me you were the one.

Who was I to question you?
You really seemed so wise.
You patiently gathered shards
Of my shredded soul despite my demise.

You held me lovingly in your arms
And sung a lullaby.

I closed my tear-filled eyes,
Bit my lip so I wouldn't cry.

Then, I clung on to you.
You vowed to never let go.
My spirit for love would have
Ceased to exist.

But you
Unexpectantly saved my soul.

Robert Uhene Maikai, Editor

155

Kimo Dunn - Sustaining love, how beautiful it is. Take it for what it is. All we need to know is how to plant the seed and to trust it will blossom bountifully.

CLEAN PRECIOUS LOVE - dedicated to my family and wife

THE NEED TO HEED - dedicated to my family and wife

MY SOUL, MY SOULMATE TENDERLY - dedicated to my family and wife

CLEAN PRECIOUS LOVE

How to make my life complete?
I send contentment and satisfaction out on a mission.
Searching for a King,
Knowing that the King is everywhere!
So amazingly grateful to have been faithful
Filled with forever grace.

Daily I will sing of the King's lovingness
In giving contentment and satisfaction yet another day,
Once away
At least, once in a lifetime.

Go to the nearest river
Wash contentment and satisfaction clean!
Soak in the water of love invested.
Then triumph again and again.

Resume being the one who creates and sends forth
Both contentment and satisfaction
Both the problem and the solution
and rejoice in the answers found.

Then go to the next river
Wash contentment and satisfaction clean!
Soak in the water of precious love!

Absorb the magical feeling of that which was lost being found.

'Oh here now Ku'uipo come now
And come to love your daily mission forevermore!

THE NEED TO HEED

There is a need to heed
the feed
on the seed of life planted
Teeing off
Not veering wrongly
In doing a good deed.

There is a need to heed
Every deed
Without greed
Or lead.
And please don't
Indeed regret a deed well done.

MY SOUL, MY SOULMATE TENDERLY

My soul, my soul,
My soulmate tenderly
For love walk towards me,
Never walk away
From tender utmost care gladly given.

Soul and Soulmate,
Delight in
Each other's presence
Sustaining each's pounding heart
Burning together evermore.

Remain in the abode of comforting love
Created by each
In each others presence
Remain in each's
Warm embrace.

Summon gratitude
For the opportunity of being with someone so special.
Comfort one another with one heart of love.
So generously benefitting both
Submerge in the moment to keep eternally close and very much
blessed.

Robert Uhene Maikai, Editor

Kaethe Kauffman (aka Cate Burns) earned a Ph.D. in Art History and is an Associate Professor of Art. She has taught at the University of California Irvine, and at Chaminade University in Honolulu among other universities. She has innovated inter-disciplinary team-taught courses such as Art and Writing and Art and Psychology. Her poems appear in VOLUTIONS - 2014 Savant Poetry Anthology, RUNNING FROM THE PACK - 2015/16 Savant Poetry Anthology, KINDRED - 2018 Savant Poetry Anthology and ENTWINED - 2019 Savant Poetry Anthology. She is the author of LIBIDO TSUNAMI: Awash with the Droll in Life (Savant 2016), novel written under the pen name Cate Burns.

WALK TO THE BEACH

UNDRESSING

THE BLUE YOUTH

SUPERIOR BEINGS

GENEROUS IN READINESS

WALK TO THE BEACH

I walk across the street, a busy city corridor where buses park
and construction cranes loom.
A white plastic bag is tied to a tree like a large Christmas
ornament, bulging into spiky shapes
Defined, I imagine, by empty food take-out boxes inside.
If it was Christmas morning, this large oddly shaped package
would be
The source of elated mystery and eager expectation.

I walk with lowered head to examine the signs people leave at
my feet.
I pick up a small circle, archetype of psychological unity.
When left to themselves with pencil and paper, schizophrenics
draw circles to soothe themselves.
I sometimes do this too.
This round latex holds the sacred male life force, expended in
an act of joy and release,
Left to bless my urban trail.

A block from home, on the beach, people leave signs of
celebration.
Frail gossamer fragments inflate with wind and blow in
abandon.
Some are clear, a watery mirror-like shape that I might gaze
into and see a new world.

Some are white, contained on three sides.

When filled with gusty trade winds, they make a bulbous shape like an unattached head.

I give chase, and capture all I can reach, for I hear the fish would be just as charmed as I

And gobble them with a fatal end.

UNDRESSING

Each decade, I undress a little at a time,
Removing more of my Invisibility Coat
Which has kept me warm most of my life,
Safe, dry and unseen.

I startle when someone notices I am in a room.
Assuming my special wrap keeps me secluded.
Each time I am recognized, I remember again;
An unknown part of me had decided to allow slow emergence.
But I'd rather cringe in a cozy hideaway.

I don't recall when I first donned a full-length quilted
Invisibility garment.
In the shady years of early childhood,
I remember cold.
Crouching behind couches, next to heating vents
And, in summer, at the tops of trees, in full sun,
Free from raucous teen-aged sisters and drunk parents.

When I hide, I savor quiet security.
No hyena shrieks from sly siblings
Who whip their feet at my ankles to send me sprawling.
No adults repeating, "You cause nothing but problems,
Kaethe."

Behind the sofa, I huddle next to our old mongrel Curly
Who adorns my face with kisses.
Atop my tall leafy dogwood tree,
I re-read Anne Frank and Little Women
Not understanding, until adulthood, how much
I need companions who know the importance of hiding.
When I cry for Anne or Beth over and over again,
I have no idea I grieve for myself.

A niggling force thrusts me into the world,
School activities, Girl Scouts,
Later, jobs, even teaching with thirty pairs of eyes examining
me.

Tight inner trusses hold me aloof,
While I play and work with others,
Yet remain astounded when anyone comments upon my
presence.

One day in my thirties, I stand before a classroom of adults.

With sudden comprehension, I realize they can see the real me.
I sometimes make mistakes and they witness my errors
And yet they return to class the next day.

At last, I understand that I must be okay.

From this tiny beginning, I begin to loosen my Invisibility
blinders.

I'm still surprised when an acquaintance spots me in a grocery
store.
The old shroud clings at times,
But I can more quickly release it.

I sometimes laugh at the relic.
It looks like Aunt Lin's woolen World War II nursing cape,
Thick and heavy, navy blue on one side, maroon on the other,
Reversible.
It loosely rests on my shoulders and
Flaps in whatever breeze pushes it, this way and that.
Sometimes it blows off and remains lost
Until I find it again.

In my ABC exercise class,
After Breast Cancer,

I quickly make friends with these survivors,
Except one.
During the last class, I don't sense the presence of a certain
young woman.
Silent and submissive, she seems long practiced in the
Invisibility Arts
And fades into the wall whenever I glance her way.

In a group of seven people, I don't perceive her for six weeks.

When I recount memories of each session,
I remember she had been at every class,
But as a vapor, ghost-like.

My chest aches for her,
Hiding with cancer.
I understand the comfort and illusory safety of solitude.
But, like me, she's in the class to gain strength.
We show up, to continue the slow undressing process.

Although it's the last class,
I must let her know I have seen her.
I hold out my hand,
"Hi, I'm Kaethe."

THE BLUE YOUTH

I wanted Mom to know who I was,
Deep inside, under expectations.
One day, at a robust fifty, working full time and raising a son,
I awoke in the morning with this strange need,
Foreign to my hectic life.

The impulse wouldn't go away
And my mind schemed.
How could I do it?
Call her on the phone?
She'd be drunk and wouldn't comprehend.
Write a letter?
The limited words would confuse and anger her.
Travel one thousand miles to visit her home?
Hung over in the mornings and sloshed by noon,
I had no opening into sober integrity,
Typical of my life with her.
Why did I want to break the barrier now?
I didn't know.

But every day an irresistible urge pushed the desire forward.
Several weeks later, on a weekend afternoon, I napped.
When I began to awaken, a beautiful blue-skinned young man
appeared

With lush black hair and green eyes.
He told me he had come to help me tell Mom the truth.
With immediate trust, I grinned, clapped my hands and cheered.

Right away, the Blue Youth gathered Mom and I together in Dad's garage,
Where my father had mended old rototillers, lawn mowers, cars and bicycles
Forty years ago when he was still alive.
I had always loved watching him transform piles of metal pieces
Into startling, roaring machines, full of purpose.

The Blue Youth told Mom the rules.
"Kaethe will tell you who she is.
"You will listen.
"You will understand."
Oddly, Mom obeyed.

We each perched on a stool in the dim, dusty two-car garage,
Facing one another in a triangle.
The Blue Youth's seat was slightly higher than ours, as if he were our mediator.

I sat delighted and stupefied in his presence.

Perhaps he was the Hindu Krishna or the Tibetan Medicine
Buddha.
I doubted I could speak, so thrilled was my tongue.
And overcome that he so perfectly expressed my heart's needs.

He turned to me,
"Kaethe, you will tell your mother exactly who you are
"And what it is like to be her daughter."
He gave me an expectant look, a cue to begin.
Without effort, my yearning spilled into space.

"Mom, I'm a quiet person who loves books.
"I was overwhelmed by the endless parties in our home.
"You were so beautiful and everyone revered you.
"I tried to copy you, to shine and sparkle,
"But always failed and felt hopeless.
"I lived in heartbreak,
"And that's what it was like to be your daughter."

Easily, I spoke in rhythms that flowed.
The last sentence became a refrain,
An end to each verse.

Poem after poem spilled from me,
How much I loved nature and the camping trips we enjoyed,
The family gatherings with songs, ukuleles, hot dogs and
bonfires.

How I tried to like her boyfriends, fiancés and husbands,
But couldn't.
In every stanza, I revealed how I adored her,
And that I ached when my worship remained unrequited.

I looked Mom in the eye as I spoke,
No desire to hurt or blame,
Simple truth.
I knew she understood, a miracle to me.

The Blue Youth nodded, encouraging both of us.
My words had become a sacred chant,
Like a resurrected ancient ceremony.
I was one of a lineage of millions of daughters who had
Performed a vital rite of passage
To show a mother her daughter's spiritual essence.

When I sang the last
"And that's what it was like to be your daughter,"
The Blue Youth declared us complete.
He bowed, then touched our shoulders before he left
While my eyes filled with tears of gratitude.
Mom and I parted with gentle pats on the arms and smiles.
I never saw her again.

I awakened from the light doze,
My craving to communicate with Mom satisfied,

My face wet with effort and appreciation of the Blue Youth,
Whether Krishna or Buddha.

One month later, Mom died suddenly, unexpectedly.
In shock, barrels of my tears ran.
But, as weeks and months passed, although sad,
I found a clear inner plateau,
Free of guilt or regret for our difficult times together.

The Blue Youth had honored my wish to abide with Mom.
He found the perfect time for us to be together in honesty,
To clean our souls' slates
Before the huge transition.
The lovely young man may have been a dream
But the help he gave was real.

SUPERIOR BEINGS

When I was a child, a teen-ager, a young woman and
middle-aged
I looked up to superior people all around me.
I assumed they could advise me how best to be an artist
Or calm my mind.

Now seventy, I find little wisdom in the outer world.
I see skilled people who have memorized medical texts,
airplane manuals, and plumbing diagrams.
How I grin when I need their help and they are there.

But I notice most folks grope in confusion,
Plumping out flesh with alcohol and starches
Or exposing themselves to bullies.
No matter how clever, legions of experts can't help us find
peace
Within our ever-changing bodies and minds.

Where did all the astute people I knew in youth disappear to?
I feel adrift without them.
In my eighth decade, I understand I had created them from
reverent desires,
Elevated them on pedestals around me
To create a false secure field.
Now it's gone.

Bereft, I want my hollow but majestic pillars back.

Instead, I search and find a few wise ones to teach me.
Yoga and meditation teachers train me to breathe into my navel
While I wait on a gurney for the surgeon to arrive.
Cells melt into such peace that when the nurse inserts the
intravenous apparatus,
I feel a small tug on the skin, no pain.

A monk teaches me to gaze, with closed eyes, up to the spot
between my eyebrows.
Like a mystic circuit-breaker switch
All thoughts cease.
In empty space, I ride on drifting colors, deep blue, magenta,
orange.
It is enough for the moment.

That instant is what I have.
It contains life force essence, strong joy and knowledge.
If in the outer world, I cling to a vampire friend,
While in the inner space, I often see my folly
And know what is right for me.
I locate the strength needed to change a bad situation.
In my center I find calm, a grounding authority within
Rather than building outer spires to lean on.

At seventy, I am grateful.

GENEROUS IN READINESS

My friends, Connie and Pat don't know each other.
Their laughter is feeble now,
But they are willing to giggle with me.

Both want to die quickly.

It's unlikely either will get her wish.
Medical science's keeps them lingering
And neither live in a state that allows human-finessed death
options.

How does a person find a graceful time to stop?
I understand Connie and Pat's journeys.
Connie suffers with three bad diseases,
Pat with spreading cancer.
And yet they laugh with me.

I ache with tenderness as I watch, support and love them.

I think of others who gave up.
And dropped into a black abyss.
A close friend, Becky, an extraverted party girl,
Announced at age seventy, she gave up all male
And most female friends.
Thrice married, this was akin to cutting out a vital organ.
She became bitter and accusatory to all.

Ditto for Mom.

With a history of husbands and fiancés galore,

Mom's distressed declaration at age eighty,

Meant she no longer knew how to live.

In Mom's opinion, the bulbous scars on her stomach

Rendered her unfit for male regard.

My tiny scars shuddered with her humiliation,

My eyes thick with tears.

No matter how much I hurt for her,

I was unable to help.

Several months later, she cooked eggs for breakfast,

But died so quickly from an exploding brain, she didn't get to eat them.

Her sister, Joanna, was ninety when she released her desire to live.

Instead of men and parties, her passion was golf.

When her arthritic hands could no longer hold the clubs,

She decided to leave

Despite the children, grandchildren and great- grandchildren

Who begged her to stay.

She stopped eating.

I see diverse ways of becoming ready to let go.

At any age,

The mental decision seems paramount
To how much suffering it spreads to others.

I often find ripe mangos on the ground,
Fallen from their mother tree.
As I enjoy their sweet juices,
I think of Connie and Pat, generous in their readiness.

Robert Uhene Maikai, Editor

Serena Saleh was born in Dearborn, Michigan, and has attended the American School of Kuwait since the beginning of her educational career and is a member at the Small Learning Community within ASK. Along with reading and poetry, Serena enjoys being a part of her competitive dance team and playing the flute and guitar. In addition to fine arts, Serena is a part of the MUN, Academic Games team, and Student Council.

MY LOVE FOR YOU

MY LOVE FOR YOU

A Romeo and Juliet poem in Juliet's Perspective

Flickering and flaming like my love for you,
They say to stay away but I linger longer,
Into your eyes, deep and mysterious as the rest of you,
Yet your smile brings me closer.

The scent of the burnt-out candle,
Is supposed to smell bad,
But it's my kind of scandal,
And the smoke fills my body,

Like the tingles, I get from seeing you,
The butterflies fluttering around,
The happiness in me made me knew,
That even though I loved you, they would frown.

NO! Our families push us away with such emotion,
But you still come back with weariness in your eyes,
I cry day and night and take the potion.
You come back thinking I died.

Waking up to the feeling of dread,
I get up and look for you
Lying next to my bed,
Is the soulless body of Romeo,

Our families wanted us apart,
No matter how fast we fled,
We both knew in our hearts,
We would love each other even if we were dead.

Robert Uhene Maikai, Editor

Cigeng Zhang from China is a freelance translator. Her poems "Calla Lily," "Twin Lotus Flowers," "A Visit to Hanshan Temple" and others have appeared in SHADOW AND LIGHT - 2017 Savant Poetry Anthology, KINDRED - Savant 2018 Poetry Anthology and ENTWINED - 2019 Savant Poetry Anthology. Her bilingual poetry collection, ROUGE IN THE WATER was published in China in 2017; her works also appear in the LOST TOWER anthologies (2014-2017) and the POETIC BOND Volumes III - IX (2013-2019).

THE COWHERD AND GIRL-WEAVER STARS

WINTER NIGHT WOODS

ELLEN

FACIAL MASK

THE COWHERD AND GIRL-WEAVER STARS

a dull pain, somehow
started in my neck
chronic pains, I thought that
must be the Hashimoto disease
did the mischief in me

pushed open the window
deep breathe for the sense of relief
a damp wind blew by
the sky of July eroded by bleak rain

Pain is the Heart of Bitter Yearning

I looked up
night misty dark
you must be unable to
see the small pouch I embroidered
just as I, could not capture
your long-gone silhouette
when flashing across the galaxy, mutely

WINTER NIGHT WOODS

A flock of crows gathered on the tall poplars in the dim moon
Black silhouettes densely clung to the curtain of mute night
I had to hold my breath and hurried up my pace
Wanting to leave the ghostly shadowy trees quickly
But I could not help looking up at the treetops now and again
What I got to see was many a little Halloween imp, weird

ELLEN

Overlooking for a century
She turned to a stone statue
A flock cf fish swimming past her
spouted foams from their mouths

Rejoicing in what she saw
Silver gulls lingered above the foams
Wings skimming across the sky
left a swift wind behind

A salty air was the taste of freedom
Foams as blue as her old dreams
The brownish freckles on her cheeks
Cute and girlish, like twinkly things

FACIAL MASK

The mud of the Dead Sea

Placed on my face and body

I turned to a dark clay sculpture

Seeing neither the flecks, scars

Nor sorrows, the type of

Camille Claudel, the lover of Rodin

I only had the dead sea mud¹

Wrapping my groan for losing you

Robert Uhene Maikai, Editor

Martin Estaban - Poetry should be sweetly savored.

SWEET SAVOR - dedicated to all my *ohana*

SWEET SAVOR

Been around here before and know the force
The pull on each captive wrongly held in thrall.

But I didn't know choice.
Sweet, rare choice
As if knowing is the same as having
But the feeling! So, good, so good.

It's so good, so good,
To be able to put forlornness aside
And once again to trust
In something, someone, anyone

A poetic savior.
A warm caring glow in the mind.

Freshly restored,
Indeed being so good, so good,
Turning everything inside out
Trading the battle, for what...?

I've forgotten, really.
Not outwardly, just within.

Mike Patelo - Sharing and caring ultimately transcends all

CARE TRANSCENDENT - dedicated to my family and those in touch who see things much better than I

TREASURE SHINING - dedicated to my family and those in touch who see things much better than I

CARE TRANSCENDENT

Care from in the heart is given unto
Whomever comes in contact.
Sharing and caring from the heart to all
Sharing and caring from the heart to all in need.

Desperation of the heart needs to be filled
The void, empty, calling
Wanting so much
That which it can not give.

Relief comes from both giving and receiving
Touching another's heart
Being touched by another's heart
The warmth and caring transcend

TREASURE SHINING

A jewel in the rough
Treasure taken from deep in the earth
Doesn't shine
Nor is it recognized.

And yet,
With loving care
It transforms into a treasure shining
That never tarnishes!

Robert Uhene Maikai, Editor

Mark Kempf - What a time, what a place of remember

EVERLASTING ARMS - dedicated to my special, lovely , treasured , cherished wife and two *ohana* daughters, son and grandchild.

EVERLASTING ARMS

I seek
high above
the Maker of the stars,
He or she who gave
first breath.

When rain falls
sunshine calls.
There is no greater love
then that above.
So light my path

Provide a refuge
for my soul.
Take me in the everlasting arms
and let me live in your abode.
Astounding is that place, is it not?

Keep your light upon me!
Regardless the circumstances
light to my path.
Pray for me, too,
if you wish.

Be kind as a beautiful morning
give courage from above.
Find me; here I am.
Extend your everlasting arms,
Bring me home.

Abram Rocky Horner - It's all about where the wind blows and the rain falls...

UNIFORMED UNCERTAINTIES - dedicated to my ohana and the many who touch our lives

A STORY THAT NEEDS UNDERSTANDING - dedicated to my ohana and the many who touch our lives

UNIFORMED UNCERTAINTIES

Not televised,
Not televised only
Just publicized,
In a time of uncertainties

Confused,
Really confused,
More un-understandable
What's happening these days.

Lost,
Not lost only
More advertised,
In a time of uniformed uncertainties

Posted
Not posted only,
More information,
True or not, no one cares.

Blown up,
But not blown up only
Just exaggerated,
But then, true or not, who cares?

A STORY THAT NEEDS UNDERSTANDING

Got to understand the story,
To understand the plan
To figure out the purpose
To discern the value
To appreciate the story.

Got to understand the story
This is what really
Needs to be done.
The whole story told
Not just in bits and pieces
In order to make an unclear decision on the matter.

Unclear? Of course!
Whatever you think may have been said --
"It happened this way!" --
It's at best a façade
Patina on the surface.

No, the story is never about the story,
It's about something never imagined
Taking place
And never known before
Somewhere between the words
In the plan

Robert Uhene Maikai, Editor

On the purpose
Of the value
Of the story.

Conner Maika'i-St. Louis - the world should always be viewed under a microscope

THE HEMISPHERE BURNS WITH GLADNESS - dedicated to my family and friends, but most importantly to my dear mother and lovely grandmother.

THE HEMISPHERE BURNS WITH GLADNESS

Yours is the beauty of creation
Wrapped into a bouquet
Manifest within a Lioness' heart.

Never give up the longing
To be ravished by tender love.

Yours is the panoply of amazing crystal colors
Sparkling clusters above the skies
Showcasing rainbows in gentle Hawaiian chants.

Ignite the flame of love.
Let it intertwine soft spoken melodies unlocking time.

Fire the hemisphere to burn in perpetual gladness.
Rare is love so powerful a chemical reaction as to give off a
sonic boom
Bursting like winter waves, calling out to all who hear.

Be forever entrenched in desires unforbidden.
Take another, another love .

What can a person hope to receive beyond love,
Mad love?
No room to falter, only overcoming.

Beneath the constant crystal lights of the Southern Sky,
In my eyes, your beauty sparkles as if one with the stars.

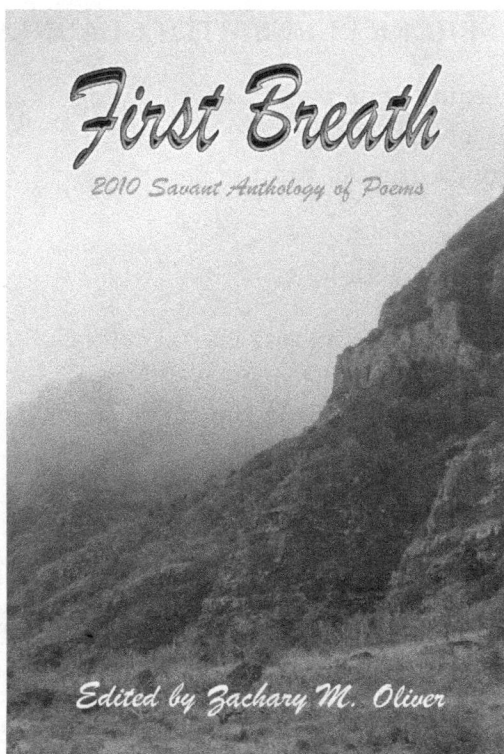

First Breath - 2010 Savant Anthology of Poems
Zachary M. Oliver (Editor)
72 pp. 5.25" x 8" Softcover
ISBN 978-0-9845552-2-2
Twenty-nine poems by ten outstanding poets and writers
selected for their outstanding merit, including Helen Doan, Erin L.
George, Jack Howard, Daniel S. Janik, Scott Mastro, Zachary M.
Oliver, Francis H. Powell, Gabjirel Ra, V. Bright Saigal and Orest
Stocco.

Robert Uhene Maikai, Editor

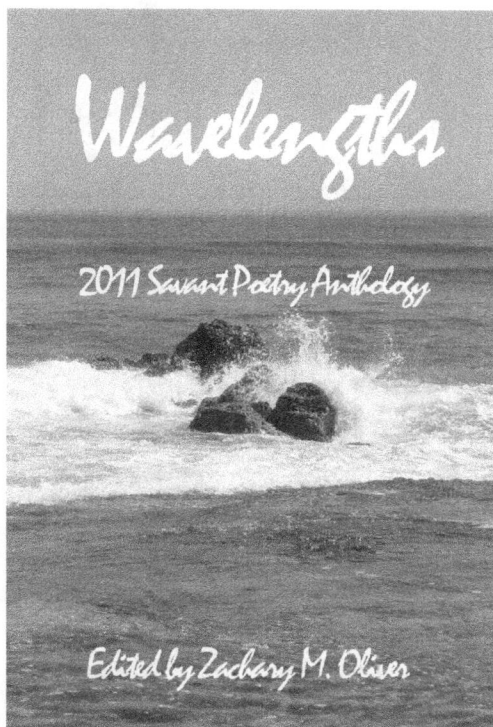

Wavelengths - 2011 Savant Poetry Anthology
Zachary M. Oliver (Editor)
102 pp. 5.25" x 8" Softcover
ISBN 978-0-9829987-6-2
Thirty-eight poems by sixteen outstanding poets and writers
including Four Arrows, Penny Lynn Cates, J. R. Coleman, Nadia Cox,
Helen Doan, Erin L George, IKO, Daniel S. Janik, Vivekanand Jha, A.
K. Kelly, Zachary M. Oliver, Cara Richardson, Michael Shorb, Jason
Sturner, Jean Yamasaki Toyama and Jeremy Ussher.

LONDON BOOK FESTIVAL AWARD

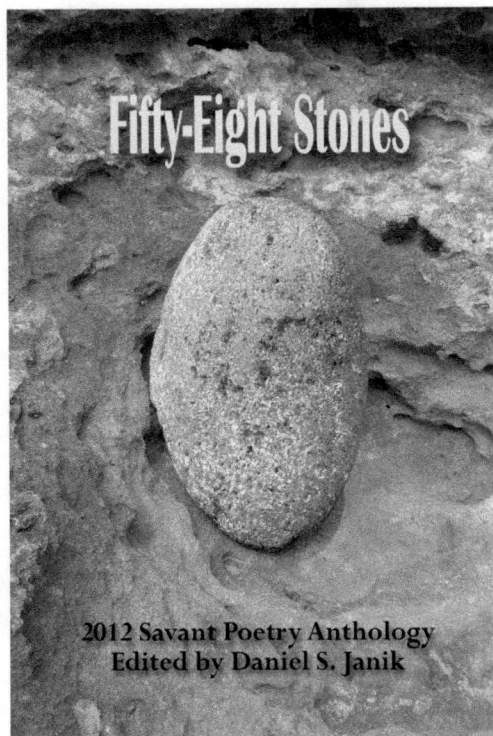

Fifty-Eight Stones - 2012 Savant Poetry Anthology
Daniel S. Janik (Editor)
128 pp. 5.25" x 8" Softcover
ISBN 978-0-9852506-5-2
Thirty-four outstanding poems by eleven exceptional and many award-winning poets including Shawn Canon, Nadia Cox, Helen Doan, David Gemmell, Richard Hookway, Daniel S. Janik, Vivekanand Jha, Doc Krinberg, Julie McKinney, Francis Powell and Jean Yamasaki Toyama.

Robert Uhene Maikai, Editor

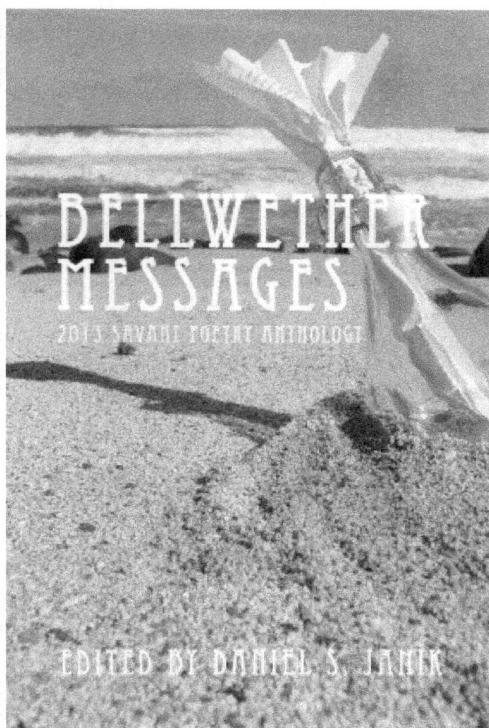

Bellwether Messages - 2013 Savant Poetry Anthology
Daniel S. Janik (Editor)
134 pp. 5.25" x 8" Softcover Pocketbook
ISBN 978-0-9886640-4-3

Thirty-two selected poems by fourteen outstanding poets including Tender Bastard, Shawn P. Canon, Natascha Hoover, IKO, Daniel S. Janik, Vivekanand Jha, Thomas Koron, Doc Krinberg, Cathal Patrick Little, Peter Mallett, Emma Myles, Ken Rasti, Uhene' and Ashley Vaughan.

LONDON BOOK FESTIVAL AWARD

Volutions - 2014 Savant Poetry Anthology
Suzanne Langford (Editor)
146 pp. 5.25" x 8" Softcover Pocketbook
ISBN 978-0-9915622-1-3
Thirty-six exceptional poems by fourteen outstanding poets including Noemi Villagrana Barragan, Elsha Bohnert, Hans Brinckmann, Helen R. Davis, K. Lauren de Boer, Duandino, Lonner F. Holden, Daniel S. Janik, Kaethe Kauffman, Suzanne Langford, Lucretia Leong, C. P. Little, Leilani Madison and Lady Mariposa.

LA, LONDON, PARIS and PACFIC RIM BOOK FESTIVAL AWARDS

Robert Uhene Maikai, Editor

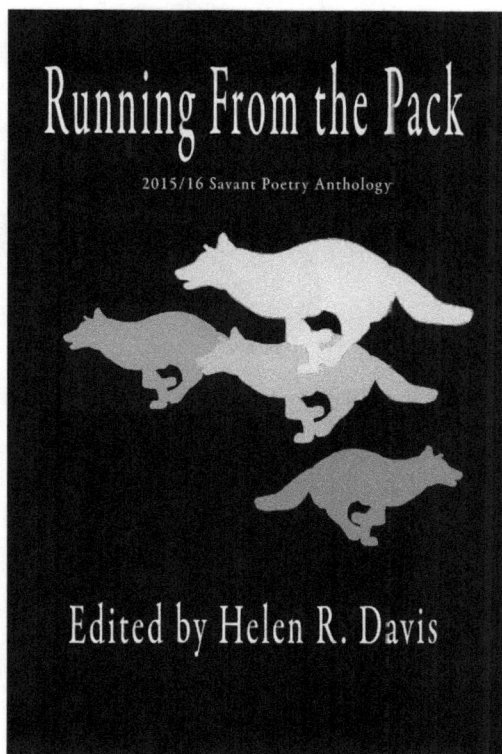

Running from the Pack - 2015/16 Savant Poetry Anthology

Helen R. Davis (Editor)
100 pp. 5.25" x 8" Softcover
ISBN 978-0-9963255-5-4

Thirty-five selected poems by fifteen outstanding poets including Dylan DiMarchi, Teuta S. Rizaj, Uhene, Marianne Smith, Danny Smith, Manal Hamad, Thomas Koron, J. Okajima, A. G. Hayes, Kelsea Kennedy, C. P. Little, Helen R. Davis, Doc Krinberg, Kaethe Kauffman and Daniel S. Janik.

PACFIC RIM BOOK FESTIVAL AWARD

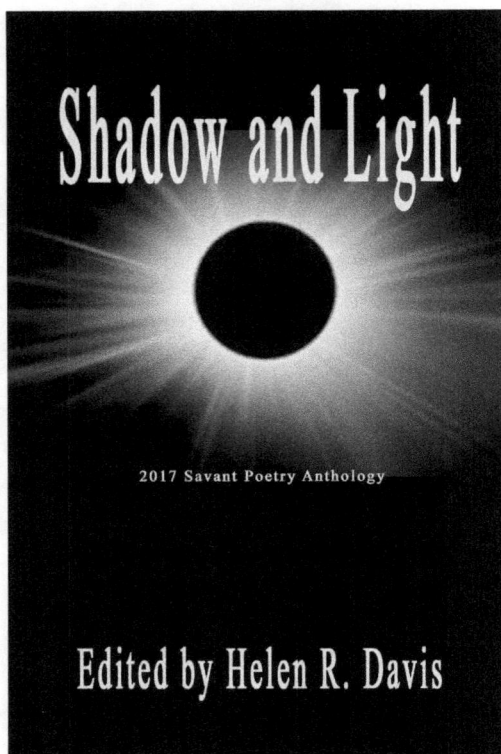

Shadow and Light - 2017 Savant Poetry Anthology
Edited by Helen R. Davis
134 pp. 5.25" x 8" Softcover Pocketbook
ISBN 978-0-9972472-8-2

Sixty-four selected poems by twenty-two outstanding poets including, in order of appearance, Rose Seaquill, Bipul Banerjee, Dr. Mike, Doc Krinberg, Jock Armour, Mr. Ben, Emily Anderson, Marianne Smith, Carolina Casas, Cigeng Zhang, Thomas Koron, Mark Daniel Seiler, Dwight Armbrust Jr, Uhene, Daniel S. Janik, Lonner F. Holden, Sara Hawley, Ihar Kazak, Barbara Bailey, V. Bright Saigal, Ken Rasti and Teuta S. Rizaj.

Robert Uhene Maikai, Editor

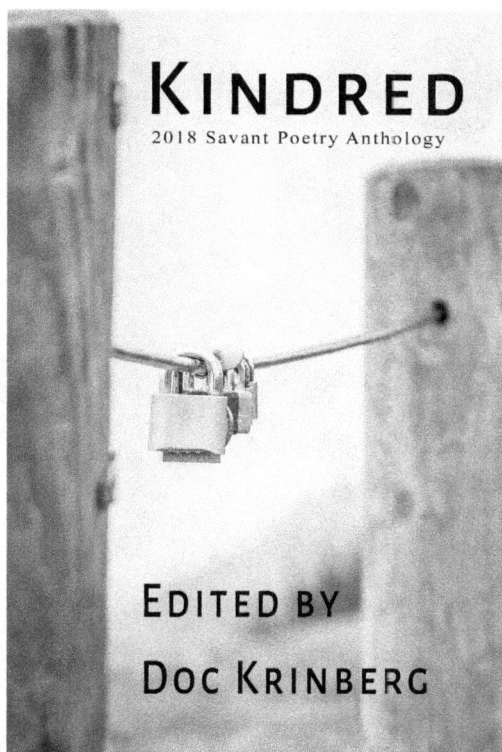

KINDRED - 2018 Savant Poetry Anthology
Edited by Doc Krinberg
110 pp - 5.25" x 8" Softcover Pocketbook
ISBN/EAN 978-0-9994633-0-7

Fifty select poems by nineteen outstanding poets including Dorothy Winslow Wright, Daniel S. Janik, Doc Krinberg, Stacey Lorinn Joy, Bipul Banerjee, Anna Banasiak, Jana Gartung, Hongri Yuan, Cigeng Zhang, Heidi Willson, Kaethe Kauffman, Irtika Kazi, Ihar Kazak, Shikeb Siddiqi, T.W. Behz, Thomas Koron, Uhene, Ken Rasti and Derek Bickerton.

Aloha La'a Kea -- Sacred Light of Love

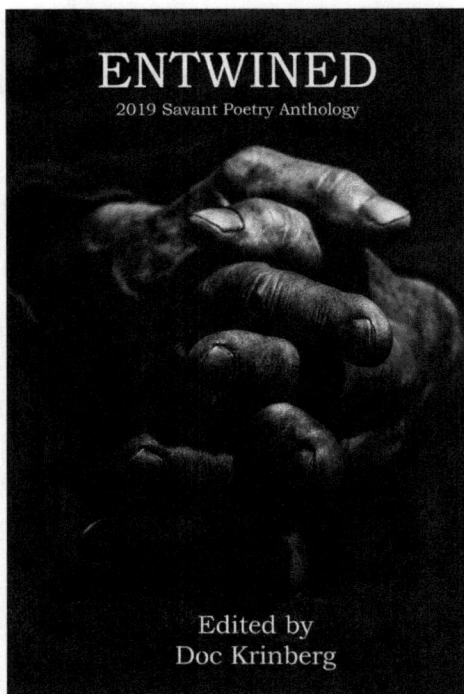

ENTWINED - 2019 Savant Poetry Anthology
Edited by Doc Krinberg
140 pp; 5.25" x 8" Softcover Pocketbook
ISBN/EAN 978-0-9994633-7-6
Suggested Retail Price $10.95

Sixty-six outstanding poems by twenty-one notable poets including Jean Toyama, Shikeb Siddiqi, Ndaba Sibanda, Thomas Koron, Sahaj Sabharwal, Ulysses Tetu, Bhupesh Chandra Karmakar, Cigeng Zhang, Daniel S. Janik, Karen T. Sisler, Robert Wood, Anna Banasiak, Kierra Donadelle, Ihar Kazak, Stacey Lorinn Joy, V. Bright Saigal, Kaethe Kauffman, Dorothy Winslow Wright, Lonner Holden, Priya Patel and Doc Krinberg.

AN AMAZON GENRE BESTSELLER

212

Robert Uhene Maikai, Editor

*If you enjoyed **Aloha La'a Kea**, consider these other fine poetic works from Savant Books and Publications:*

Savant Single-Poet Poetry Collections
Footprints, Smiles and Little White Lies by Daniel S. Janik
The Illustrated Middle Earth by Daniel S. Janik
Last and Final Harvest by Daniel S. Janik

Aignos Single-Poet Poetry Collections
Iwana by Alvaro Leiva
Prepositions by Jean Yamasaki Toyama

...as well as these other fine books from Savant Books and Publications:

Essay, Essay, Essay by Yasuo Kobachi
Aloha from Coffee Island by Walter Miyanari
Footprints, Smiles and Little White Lies by Daniel S. Janik
The Illustrated Middle Earth by Daniel S. Janik
Last and Final Harvest by Daniel S. Janik
A Whale's Tale by Daniel S. Janik
Tropic of California by R. Page Kaufman
Tropic of California (the companion music CD) by R. Page Kaufman
The Village Curtain by Tony Tame
Dare to Love in Oz by William Maltese
The Interzone by Tatsuyuki Kobayashi
Today I Am a Man by Larry Rodness
The Bahrain Conspiracy by Bentley Gates
Called Home by Gloria Schumann
First Breath edited by Z. M. Oliver
The Jumper Chronicles by W. C. Peever
William Maltese's Flicker by William Maltese
My Unborn Child by Orest Stocco
Last Song of the Whales by Four Arrows
Perilous Panacea by Ronald Klueh
Falling but Fulfilled by Zachary M. Oliver
Mythical Voyage by Robin Ymer
Hello, Norma Jean by Sue Dolleris
Charlie No Face by David B. Seaburn
Number One Bestseller by Brian Morley
My Two Wives and Three Husbands by S. Stanley Gordon
In Dire Straits by Jim Currie
Wretched Land by Mila Komarnisky
Who's Killing All the Lawyers? by A. G. Hayes
Ammon's Horn by G. Amati
Wavelengths edited by Zachary M. Oliver
Communion by Jean Blasiar and Jonathan Marcantoni
The Oil Man by Leon Puissegur
Random Views of Asia from the Mid-Pacific by William E. Sharp
The Isla Vista Crucible by Reilly Ridgell
Blood Money by Scott Mastro
In the Himalayan Nights by Anoop Chandola

Robert Uhene Maikai, Editor

On My Behalf by Helen Doan
Traveler's Rest by Jonathan Marcantoni
Chimney Bluffs by David B. Seaburn
The Loons by Sue Dolleris
Light Surfer by David Allan Williams
The Judas List by A. G. Hayes
Path of the Templar—Book 2 of The Jumper Chronicles by W. C. Peever
The Desperate Cycle by Tony Tame
Shutterbug by Buz Sawyer
Blessed are the Peacekeepers by Tom Donnelly and Mike Munger
Bellwether Messages edited by D. S. Janik
The Turtle Dances by Daniel S. Janik
The Lazarus Conspiracies by Richard Rose
Purple Haze by George B. Hudson
Imminent Danger by A. G. Hayes
Lullaby Moon (CD) by Malia Elliott of Leon & Malia
Volutions edited by Suzanne Langford
In the Eyes of the Son by Hans Brinckmann
The Hanging of Dr. Hanson by Bentley Gates
Flight of Destiny by Francis Powell
Elaine of Corbenic by Tima Z. Newman
Ballerina Birdies by Marina Yamamoto
More More Time by David B. Seabird
Crazy Like Me by Erin Lee
Cleopatra Unconquered by Helen R. Davis
Valedictory by Daniel Scott
The Chemical Factor by A. G. Hayes
Quantum Death by A. G. Hayes
Running from the Pack edited by Helen R. Davis
Big Heaven by Charlotte Hebert
Captain Riddle's Treasure by GV Rama Rao
All Things Await by Seth Clabough
Tsunami Libido by Cate Burns
Finding Kate by A. G. Hayes
The Adventures of Purple Head, Buddha Monkey and...by Erik Bracht
In the Shadows of My Mind by Andrew Massie
The Gumshoe by Richard Rose
Cereus by Z. Roux
Shadow and Light edited by Helen R. Davis
The Solar Triangle by A. G. Hayes

215

Aloha La'a Kea -- Sacred Light of Love

A Real Daughter by Lynne McKelvey
StoryTeller by Nicholas Bylotas
Bo Henry at Three Forks by Daniel D. Bradford
One Night in Bangkok by Keith R. Rees
Navel of the Sea by Elizabeth McKague
68 Via Condotti: Book One - Eternity Ltd by A. G. Hayes
Critical Writing:Stories as Phenomena by Jamie Dela Cruz
Truth and Tell Travel the Solar System by Helen R. Davis
The COMPLETE Koski & Falk by A. G. Hayes
Leon & Malia's Island Music (CD) by Leon & Malia

Coming Soon:

Honeymoon Forever: Find Love, Keep Love by R. Page Kaufman
Hawaii Kids' Music (Vol 1) (CD) by Leon & Malia

http://www.savantbooksandpublications.com

Robert Uhene Maikai, Editor

...and these from our imprint, Aignos Publishing:

The Dark Side of Sunshine by Paul Guzzo
Cazadores de Libros Perdidos by German William Cabasssa Barber [Spanish]
The Desert and the City by Derek Bickerton
The Overnight Family Man by Paul Guzzo
There is No Cholera in Zimbabwe by Zachary M. Oliver
John Doe by Buz Sawyers
The Piano Tuner's Wife by Jean Yamasaki Toyama
An Aura of Greatness by Brendan P. Burns
Polonio Pass by Doc Krinberg
Iwana by Alvaro Leiva
University and King by Jeffrey Ryan Long
The Surreal Adventures of Dr. Mingus by Jesus Richard Felix Rodriguez
Letters by Buz Sawyers
In the Heart of the Country by Derek Bickerton
El Camino De Regreso by Maricruz Acuna [Spanish]
Prepositions by Jean Yamasaki Toyama
Deep Slumber of Dogs by Doc Krinberg
Saddam's Parrot by Jim Currie
Beneath Them by Natalie Roers
Chang the Magic Cat by A. G. Hayes
Illegal by E. M. Duesel
Island Wildlife: Exiles, Expats and Exotic Others by Robert Friedman
The Winter Spider by Doc Krinberg
The Princess in My Head by J. G. Matheny
Comic Crusaders by Richard Rose
I'll Remember by Clif McCrady
The Edge of Madness by Raymond Gaynor

Coming Soon:

The City and the Desert by Derek Bickerton
For Now, Our Written Love Will Have to Do by Cheryl L. Woods

http://www.aignospublishing.com

217

www.ingramcontent.com/pod-product-compliance
Lightning Source LLC
Chambersburg PA
CBHW060236050426
42448CB00009B/1460